HV5066.H68

55

HOWARD
DID I HAVE A GOOD TIME?

DATE DUE

WITHDRAWN FROM THE EVAN'S
LIBRARY AT FMCC

DATE DUE			
APR 15 '81	DEC 04		
OCT 28 '81	NOV 20 '97		
DEC 14 '81	DEC 16 '98		
DEC 9 '82			
MAY 13 '83			
DEC 7 '83			
NOV 20 '85			
DEC 14 '87			
MAR 9			
MAR 22			
DEC 18 '89			

FULTON MONTGOMERY COMMUNITY
COLLEGE LIBRARY

Did I Have a Good Time?

Did I Have a Good Time?
ଏ Teenage Drinking

by Marion Howard, Ph.D.
Assisted by Gerry Bennett, R.N., M.S.N.

CONTINUUM / New York

1980
The Continuum Publishing Corporation
815 Second Avenue, New York, N.Y. 10017

Copyright © 1980 by Marion Howard.
All rights reserved. No part of this book may be
reproduced, stored in a retrieval system,
or transmitted, in any form or by any means,
electronic, mechanical, photocopying, recording,
or otherwise, without the written permission
of The Continuum Publishing Corporation.
Printed in the United States of America

Library of Congress Cataloging in Publication Data
Howard, Marion, 1936–
Did I have a good time?
SUMMARY: Follows the lives of three young people,
with typical problems, whose encounters with alcohol
change their lives.
1. Children—United States—Alcohol use—Juvenile
literature. [1. Alcohol. 2. Alcoholism]
I. Bennett, Gerry, joint author. II. Title.
HV5066.H68   613.8′1   80-17654
ISBN 0-8264-0017-5

Contents

Introduction **ix**
Chapter 1 / Jesse—Beginnings **1**
Chapter 2 / Christine—Beginnings **6**
Chapter 3 / Penni—Beginnings **13**
Chapter 4 / Jesse—Into It **19**
Chapter 5 / Christine—Into It **30**
Chapter 6 / Penni—Into It **46**
Chapter 7 / Jesse—Changes **59**
Chapter 8 / Christine—Changes **69**
Chapter 9 / Penni—Changes **88**
Chapter 10 / Jesse—More **101**
Chapter 11 / Christine—More **111**
Chapter 12 / Penni—More **124**
Chapter 13 / Jesse—Choices **130**
Chapter 14 / Christine—Choices **144**
Chapter 15 / Penni—Choices **154**
Resources **161**

To my father—a rare and wonderful man

Introduction

For some groups in our society, ideal drinking behavior is not drinking at all. For other groups, moderate drinking behavior is acceptable. For yet others, occasional heavy drinking or even frequent heavy drinking is permissible.

Therefore, for an adolescent, deciding about drinking behavior becomes compounded by the multiplicity of attitudes about what is "right," "normal," or "acceptable." That the adolescent cannot avoid confronting such choices is clear from the fact that close to three-quarters of American men report drinking at least once a year, and well over half of American women do the same. Recent studies indicate 93 percent of all high school seniors have tried alcohol at one time or another. Moreover, surveys show that the age at which Americans begin to drink is dropping. The average age is now thirteen. Thus more young people are making such choices earlier. It is reasonable to assume as children begin to drink more at an earlier age, alcohol problems among the young will increase. Indeed, currently 3.3 million adolescents fourteen to seventeen years of age have significant problems associated with chronic alcohol consumption.

This book is an attempt to help young people realize that learning about alcohol is important and that the decisions they make can have serious, even life-impacting consequences. It is an attempt to help them begin to understand some of the fine lines between "normal" drinking, problem drinking, and alcoholism.

Introduction

Did I Have a Good Time? is a fictional account of three very different young people. The story follows them through initial encounters with alcohol to the point at which alcohol causes some significant change in their lives. The problems the young people face—dating and drinking, making decisions about going along with the crowd, getting money to drink, telling their parents, riding in cars with people who drink—are typical of those faced by young people. Each of the young people, however, handles his or her problem in a different way, thus illustrating the range of experiences young people may have.

Did I Have a Good Time is intended to reassure young people that they are not alone in their feelings and experiences about drinking. Information and alternatives they may not have considered are pointed out. Ultimately, I hope that this book will help young people make better choices about drinking behavior.

The book is also intended to help adults become more familiar with the diverse needs young people have as they are exposed to drinking in American society. The purpose of the commentary which runs throughout the story is to clarify issues and add information of interest to teenagers, their parents, and those in the helping professions.

I am grateful to Dr. T. Berry Brazelton of Harvard University who first developed the format used in this book and whose encouragement led to its successful adoption in my first book: *Only Human: Teenage Pregnancy and Parenthood*. I also wish to acknowledge my indebtedness to Gerry Bennett, R.N., M.S.N. without whose help this book would not have been possible and to Diane Kelley, R.N., Donna Woolfe, Pharm. D., and Christine Vourakis, R.N., M.N. for the time they spent in reading drafts and making comments. A special thank you must go to my family for their patience and support.

Marion Howard
School of Medicine
Emory University
Atlanta, Georgia

1 ❧ Jesse—Beginnings

Jesse sat up in bed and looked out the window. Not that there was anything to see. The bare gray boards of the neighbor's house filled the view. Jesse had liked it better when the house's paint had first started to peel off. Sometimes it flaked off in weird patterns: a camel stepping on a turtle's back, a giant worm coming out of a moldy apple, a girl with her behind in the air. Now there were just a few strips of paint left—dull, dull, dull. The only thing left to see out the window was whether or not it was raining.

Jesse thought about getting back down under the blanket and dreaming up an adventure. In his adventures, Jesse was always a hero. It was like watching a movie with himself in it. Recently he'd been putting a lot of sex in his movies. But Jesse's mother didn't like his staying in bed that much. If she butted in before his adventure was done, it would really anger him, maybe even leave him hung up. Better not to start.

Jesse knew it was late already. He could hear the television playing one of those stupid quiz shows. Jesse never would understand how his mother could watch all those people screaming and yelling, particularly in the morning. Dull, dull, dull.

Jesse climbed out of bed and headed toward the bathroom. He stumbled over the clothes that he had left on the floor by the bed the night before. His mother hated it when Jesse slept in his clothes. But Jesse hated the too short pajamas he had so he mostly just crawled into bed bare at night. Stupid clothes.

Jesse managed to get in and out of the bathroom without looking in the mirror. It was difficult enough to see his own angular face when he was feeling good let alone when he just got up. Then he walked slowly to the kitchen.

"Well, his majesty has arrived," his mother said, taking another drag on her cigarette and then crushing it out in her coffee cup. "I suppose you'd like me to get up and fix your majesty some breakfast."

"Ah mom," Jesse said, glancing sideways at the people jumping up and down on the small television on the counter.

"The way you come and go," his mother continued, "you'd think you didn't owe anybody anything. Well, you're not going to like this Jess but I'm going to tell you something! Today you're going to stay home and help me clean up this dump."

Jesse looked at his mother. There were dark circles under her eyes. Her hair had not been combed. He wondered what he should say. Some days he'd talk back at her but today he just didn't feel like it. "Whatever you say," he mumbled.

"Don't talk back to me!" His mother poked her finger at him. "It's your attitude. You're going to get in trouble someday, bad trouble, 'cause of your attitude."

"All right, mom," Jesse mumbled turning away.

"Don't you go 'yes mamm'in' me," his mother said. Then something on the television caught her eye and she turned to look.

Jesse went over to the cupboard and took down a box of cereal. It was light and he figured there really wasn't quite enough for a full bowl. However, it would be quick and then he could get on with whatever she was going to put him through.

"Look at that! Don't that beat all!" The tone of Jesse's

mother's voice changed. "That woman just won herself a new car, a whole kitchen full of stuff, and a trip to California to boot."

Jesse saw his mother's eyes brighten momentarily. He looked at the television. He suspected his mother saw herself jumping around, hugging the announcer, being excited over all those things. There wasn't any real life way she was going to have those things but he could see she was dreaming she could get them through some magic of television.

Jesse tried to picture his mother on one of those shows. If she had to be on before breakfast, she'd hardly have energy to come up with the answers. And if she was on after lunch—well, depending.... He pictured his mother as he had often seen her, flushed and sparkley eyed—and smelling like booze. He saw her giggling like a kid over winning a year's supply of laundry soap. And then that image passed. He saw his mother swaying as she tried to press the buzzer to get out her answer and then he saw her slump over her contestant stand—dead drunk.

The cereal bowl in Jesse's hand came into focus. He walked over to the table and set it down. "You heard from Tom?" he asked, trying to take advantage of the change in his mother's mood.

Tom was Jesse's older brother. Tom had gotten out—just one day packed up and left. Said he wasn't going to rot here any more. Said he was going to get out and see the world and *be somebody*. Since then they'd heard from him once—he had said he was in the army in Texas someplace and he'd soon be going to Asia or Europe.

Jesse thought his brother was just about the greatest person in the whole world. When Jesse was little, his brother had always stuck up for him in any kind of trouble. He'd covered up for him with his mom. He'd fought other kids for him. He'd shown him all the secret places to hide in the neighborhood. He'd taught him ball throwing and running and climbing. Jesse missed Tom terribly.

I'll get out too someday. I'm going to get out of here too—maybe even soon, Jesse thought. But then he looked at his mother. How could you love somebody and hate somebody so much at the same time? If he went, who would look after his mom? Jesse tried to have as little to do as possible with his mother. Yet so many times, she couldn't get along without him he knew. Sometimes she'd be in an alcoholic fog for a week. She'd leave stove burners on, pass out with a lighted cigarette in her hand, or make trouble with the neighbors. Once or twice the police had even come around when the neighbors had complained. He'd have to make excuses or promise she wouldn't do whatever it was any more. Sometimes it seemed like he was the parent and she was the kid. Fourteen years old and a parent!

In the United States, drinking among adults is common. Currently sixty-nine percent of adults drink at least once a year. People who never drink or who are heavy drinkers are in the minority. However, there are at least 10 million adults who are alcoholics or who drink to excess. Only three to five percent of the alcoholic drinkers are homeless people living in skid row areas. The vast majority live in families where their alcoholic lives affect family, friends, and community. For each alcoholic person, on the average, the lives of four other people are deeply affected. Moreover, each year alcoholism is associated with approximately 23,000 traffic deaths, with 15,000 killings and 10,000 suicides, and with 35,000 deaths from alcohol-associated diseases.

"Nope," his mother said.

Jesse was startled at the sound of her voice. Then he remembered that he'd asked her about Tom. He understood Tom's going but he didn't understand Tom's not ever calling or writing. He didn't want to believe Tom didn't care any more but sometimes it was hard. He needed to know Tom still cared. He needed to know that Tom's getting out didn't mean he didn't care.

"Now," said his mother switching off the television with determination. "Let's see if we can do something with this dump. I expect you to start in the kitchen and work toward the living room. And no *if's, and's* or *but's*. I'll start in the living room."

Jesse watched his mother go into the living room, heard a few papers being shoved together, and then it was quiet. He knew she had lain down on the couch. He looked at the pile of dishes and cigarette butts in the sink. If she still needed to sleep last night's booze off, his mother would be asleep in another few minutes. That left the whole house for him to clean. For a minute, he looked at the door. I could just go out and keep on going. But then slowly he turned and began taking the dishes out of the sink. *God damn it, Tom. It isn't fair of you. It just isn't fair.*

2 ∾ Christine—Beginnings

"One, two, three, four. One, two, three, four. No. Point your toes, girls. Now, one, two, three, four. One, two, three, four."

Christine gracefully circled her arms over her head, stepped lightly on her toes, and gracefully extended one leg behind her. Out of the corner of her eye, she could see eleven other girls, their black leotards and white shoes moving in unison with hers. She turned lightly and like the others could see her reflection in the dance studio's giant mirror. Christine liked her image. Her brown hair curled softly around her face framing her delicate features. There were other pretty girls in the dance class, of course, but she was satisfied she could compete with any of them.

"Now, one, two, three, turn." The dance teacher's voice was rhythmic.

Christine turned and stepped lightly on her toes again. She loved the feeling of being in control of her body, of having her legs and feet respond to her commands. She wished she could keep this feeling forever.

"All right girls, that's all for today," the dance teacher called. "You need to watch your pirouettes. Keep practicing them this week. The fall recital will come sooner than you think. And don't forget. You need to get the money in for your costumes the beginning of next month."

"I feel like I need a shower," a voice said. Christine turned. It was Kay. "That heat outside is going to make me stink all the way home."

Christine smiled. Kay did not put things in the most delicate way. But Kay was one of Christine's best friends. Their birthdays were on the same day and that had made them like each other from the beginning. Both girls pulled summer skirts over their leotards and changed shoes.

"I think I'll just jump into the pool when I get home and swim it off," said Christine.

"Lucky you," replied Kay. "You get to go home in an air-conditioned car to a swimming pool and I got to take the hot old bus and baby-sit my sister so my mom can get her hair done."

"Wanna come over later and go swimming?" said Christine.

"No, after my Mom gets her hair done, we're supposed to go to my grandmother's house—she's having a carport sale and my mother promised we'd help with the selling."

"Oh, OK," said Christine. Actually selling stuff at a carport sale sounded more interesting than sitting by the pool. She also felt a twinge of jealousy at Kay's going to her grandmother's.

Christine's parents had met at college, married, and moved to this city where they had no relatives. All Christine's relatives were scattered around other states. There was no one even within a day's drive. Kay was always doing something with one relative or another. Kay took her relatives for granted and sometimes even complained about them. Christine believed Kay never seemed to realize it was something special to have "family" around.

"Well, see you soon," said Christine.

A blast of heat attacked Christine as soon as she stepped outside the door. She looked for her mother's car.

"Hey, look Christine." Another girl touched Christine's arm. "There's my mom with your mom."

Christine glanced at Sandra, the girl who had called to her, and then in the direction she pointed. Sandra was right. Their mothers were together. Both girls ran over to the car eager to get in out of the heat.

"Hi! Get in girls. How was dance?" Sandra's mother reached around and opened the car's rear door.

"OK," Sandra and Christine responded sliding in.

"Mildred and I had lunch together at Sanoff's," Christine's mother said turning around so she could see the girls. "Marvelous shrimp."

The strong smell of whiskey sours floated back to the girls as she spoke. Christine poked Sandra. But both girls kept innocent looks on their faces. Christine's mother turned back in her seat and started the car. She said something witty to Sandra's mother and they both laughed gaily. Christine poked Sandra again. Their mothers had obviously had more than shrimp and their high spirits amused the girls. Sandra and Christine listened to the chatter in the front seat for a while and then began to talk to one another.

How parents drink has a strong influence on the way their children will drink (both in adolescence and in later life). Parents who drink can set positive examples by: following a specific drink limit, drinking mainly at meals, sipping slowly, and accepting alcoholic beverages only in circumstances which do not involve work, driving, or other situations that do not mesh well with drinking. Parents further can help prevent alcoholic problems among their children by demonstrating that alcohol is not necessary to enjoy life. Family members can share activities which have drug free "highs" such as sports, crafts, games, and good discussions, thus helping to reduce unhealthy dependence on alcohol during leisure time. Parents who have problems with drinking may choose, for their children's sake as well as their own, not to drink at all. Parents who do not drink, however, should know that this practice does not change the need to educate their children about alcohol. Some children who have parents who don't drink, later develop problem drinking probably because there was no example of social drinking to follow.

"Guess where I'm going Saturday night!" said Sandra.
"Where?" asked Christine.
"To the Danvers' party!"
"You are?" Christine was really surprised. The Danvers were the leaders of the "horsies." Christine called them "horsies" because they were the people who had horses that they bred, trained, and showed at horse shows. The "horsies" lives were very much centered on horses. It took a lot of money—$15,000 for a single colt was not unusual—so the "horsies" were definitely rich. Their parties even seemed to center around horses. Whenever the Southeastern Horse Show was held, there were always parties and balls. The Danvers were the most exclusive and "best" of the horsies—whatever that meant.

"Yes," said Sandra and Christine could tell she was excited.

"But who are you going with?" Christine was puzzled. No one in their age group was connected with the Danvers. The Danvers' kids were all older.

"Mark Geigy."

"Mark Geigy?" Christine was really surprised. "But he's a senior."

"I know. Isn't it just too neat?" Sandra giggled.

Christine took another look at Sandra. Sandra was one of Christine's many friends. Sandra was pretty and one of the sophomore cheerleaders at school just like Christine. Christine had always thought she and Sandra were rather alike but now she looked at Sandra trying to see what new advantage Sandra had.

Christine was dying to ask Sandra "how come" Mark had asked her. But she thought it might sound like a put down so she didn't. Instead she said, "but isn't that going to be a party with all older kids and grownups?"

"Yes," said Sandra. "I just hope I do OK. I've been to parties at the country club with grownups but not a party like this."

Christine knew what Sandra meant. Their parents belonged to the same country club. They had been going to those parties ever since they got too old for baby-sitters at home. There were always nonalcoholic drinks for the kids.

Most often they ended up playing Ping-pong or shooting pool in the recreation rooms downstairs while the parents drank or danced upstairs. But the Danvers' parties were different. They never had younger kids and they were a very sophisticated set.

Sandra chattered on. "At first my mom wasn't sure whether or not to let me go. Dad and mom talked a long time. I wasn't supposed to hear. 'Our little girl is growing up,' Dad said."

Christine smiled at that. Parents always never seemed to know just how old their kids were. One minute they treated you like you were all grown up and supposed to behave in the most mature way, and the next minute they were saying you weren't old enough.

"Finally mom said something about she supposed they shouldn't ruin my 'big chance' so I ought to be allowed to go." Although Sandra made a face when she said "big chance," they both knew what Sandra's mother meant.

The grownups all felt the Danvers were a big item in the county. The Danvers family had lived in the county a long time and had "power." Christine didn't quite understand how it worked but she knew that if a judge or some other official wanted to be elected, they had to get the blessings of the Danvers first. Mr. Danvers was on the hospital board and a bunch of other things all of which added up to the fact that when he talked people listened.

"Anyway, mom got me this gorgeous dress," Sandra continued. "I mean really gorgeous. It makes me look at least two years older. It's cut with the sleeves. . . ."

Christine's mind wandered. She wondered what a Danvers' party was really like. Suddenly she felt young and not very special sitting beside Sandra. She was glad when they pulled up at Sandra's house and Sandra and her mother got out.

"Sit up front with me, Christine," Christine's mother patted the seat beside her. "That way we can talk on the way home."

"No thanks, mom," said Christine. "I'm too sticky from dancing to move. I'll just sit here."

"C'mon up, Christine, I've barely seen you this week. I'd like to talk to you." Her mother's extra good mood caused her to miss the frown that was on Christine's face.

"No thanks, mom," Christine said. Then she added somewhat impatiently, "C'mon. Let's just go. I really need to get home and get out of this sticky leotard."

"OK," her mother answered, still cheerful. "You just missed a chance to have some sparkling conversation with your charming mother." She leaned over and pulled the front door closed and began driving.

Christine settled back in the seat. Her mom was right. She hadn't seen her all week. Christine had swim practice every morning. She was on the country club swim team and the coach insisted on daily practice. Then she had art lessons on Monday and Wednesday afternoon, ballet lessons on Tuesday afternoon, riding lessons on Friday. Thursday was the only afternoon she had free. However, as often as not, her mother wasn't home on Thursday.

Christine sometimes wondered about her family. They lived in the same house but they rarely seemed to meet. Discussions most often consisted of information about who was going where, who was to be home when, and who was to make arrangements for what where. Christine's dad was as bad as her mother, even worse. When he wasn't at the office or away on a trip, he was getting together with this person or that person. It seemed Christine mainly saw him when he had some business client to dinner and wanted to show off his family. Christine used to like those dinners because her dad was a very interesting man and he always put his best foot forward. On the other hand at those dinners she never really got to talk to him. Recently she had begun to resent being "on show." However, her mother didn't seem to mind; her mother actually appeared to revel in it. At times Christine wondered how her mother could be content being used liked that.

Christine's mother turned into their drive but she didn't shut off the car's motor. Instead she turned around in her seat to face Christine. "Now I've got to go to the travel agency this afternoon to see if I can't straighten out the Labor Day trip for us. I don't know why they booked your Dad and me on such a late flight. Do you want to come with me? If you do, I'll wait till you change."

"No," said Christine.

"All right, dear," her mother said. "I'm going to go now then. I've got a few other errands but I'll be home in time for dinner. If Mrs. Simpson calls, tell her I've got the membership list she wanted. And if Alexander calls me back, tell him that it's the flowered chair I want recovered and ask him to look for that plum-colored material I saw in the sample book last week."

"Yes, mother. Membership list and plum-colored material," Christine said. She got out of the car.

"I love you," her mother called out the car window as she backed out the drive. She flashed Christine a happy smile and drove off.

"OK mom," Christine waved her hand in a limp gesture.

Christine turned and sighed. She lived in a pretty home, they had enough money to feel good about their lives, they were accepted, busy, even popular but it all lacked something. That thought had occurred to her off and on but today it was particularly strong. Then she thought again of Sandra. Maybe it was Sandra's going to the Danvers' party that made her feel the way she did. She wished Kay wasn't at the carport sale.

Christine looked at the empty house and then started toward it. Maybe she could think of something to make the time go quickly until her mom or dad got home.

3 ◌ Penni—Beginnings

Penni sat on the edge of her bed. Well, it was about time to get going. She looked at the bottle in one hand and the glass in the other. She gave a smile to the bottle as if they shared a secret. "I'll see you later," she said.

Penni set the glass on the floor, picked up the screw cap, and carefully put it on the bottle. She turned it extra tight. From experience she knew if she didn't do it right, the liquid would spill out making a stinking mess while she was gone. She had to lay the bottle on its side in the suitcase she kept under her bed. There was no place to stand it up without having it discovered.

Penni pulled out the suitcase, put the bottle inside, and then shoved the suitcase back. She paused a moment longer, a smile on her face. Then she picked up the glass and stood up. She walked out the door and down the hall into the bathroom. She rinsed out the glass and put it back in its holder. Then she took out her toothbrush and toothpaste. She hated this part. Having the peppermint gunk in your mouth after that nice smooth liquid, took away some from the nice effect. However, she had to get rid of the smell so she grimaced and brushed away. One nice thing about brushing: it didn't take away from the good feelings inside.

In America, the average age at which people begin to drink is getting younger. It is now thirteen. In particular the proportion of young women who drink has risen sharply. Approximately 3.3 million adolescents (fourteen to seventeen age group) have significant problems associated with drinking alcohol. Research shows that those who begin drinking at an earlier age are more likely than others to be heavy drinkers both as teenagers and as adults.

"Sugar baby, you're the one," she hummed as she wiped her mouth with the towel. "Sugar baby, gonna have some fun." She took one final quick look in the mirror. Then she walked through the apartment and out the door, pausing only long enough to put a ribbon with a door key on it around her neck.

Penni's brother who was six years younger than she was, was in church camp for two weeks so Penni was free. With her mom working, when Freddie was at home, Penni had to watch out for him—whatever that meant. He did pretty much what he wanted anyway. But for two whole weeks Penni wouldn't have to worry. She set off in the direction of the shopping center.

Neat-o day, she thought and jumped up on the cement retainer wall surrounding the flowers beds outside their apartment building. The wall took her around away from the direction she was going. Nevertheless she followed it until she met the apartment building wall.

"Out of my way, wall!" She paused. "Didn't you hear what I said? Out of my way, wall." She waved her hand. "Won't move, huh, well, take that!" Penni put up her hands like a prize fighter. "Take that too!" She pretended to box the wall. "Uh, oh," Penni said suddenly putting her hands on the wall and pretending to hold it up. "Steady or you'll let a lot of people down." She gradually took her hands away. "I'll spare you this time, but remember I'll be back. Heh!"

Penni tossed her head in the air and jumped off the wall, a smile on her face. When she landed, however, only one foot came down squarely, the other turned sideways. She stumbled forward flailing her arms to keep her balance. "Fuckin' wall," she said angrily. Even though there was no one to see her, she felt painfully embarrassed.

Penni turned toward the shopping center. Her good mood was ruined. Damn it. She'd looked forward to these two weeks. As she walked along, however, her buoyant spirits gradually returned. By the time she arrived at the shopping center, she felt almost as good as she had when she left the apartment.

It was still early, the stores hadn't opened yet. Not that that was the main object of coming anyway; the shopping mall was just the place to go. All the kids came here sooner or later. Of course, some, like Penni, came more often than others. Penni walked around the huge closed building toward the far parking lot. No one there. If anyone had come, they'd be sitting on a casing surrounding one of the few trees. "Well, I might as well be the first one." Penni thought.

The sun had started to get hot already so the shade of a tree would be welcome. Penni slowly crossed the parking lot toward one of the trees. As she walked, she watched cars turn in toward the mall and then circle around to find their favorite parking spot. From her vantage point they looked like bees coming to their hive. The more Penni thought, the more she liked that idea. In her mind, the mall became a huge bee hive. She watched more cars arrive. Each car was a buzzing bee returning with honey. No, it had to be better than that—returning with . . . money . . . they'd been sent out to gather. Hmm. She liked the idea. Let's see. The cash registers in the mall were the combs in which they put their honey money. Hmmmm. More bees with the money. Hummmm, zzzzz. The cars were arriving at a greater rate. More money, more money.

Let's see. Hives had a queen bee and the other bees went

out and got the pollen for her. Penni smiled. She pictured herself standing on top of the mall wearing a huge flowing gold cape. More money, she yelled. More money. Get back out there and get more money. She pointed her finger. More money, she yelled. The motors of hundreds of cars roared obediently, slaves to her desires for money. Soon there was a monumental traffic jam as thousands of cars tried to get in and out of the parking lot. But the image gradually faded.

Maybe there was a hidden money monster who lived beneath the mall, too fat and swollen with greed to ever get out. She could hear him groaning and slurping as he devoured the money. No. She didn't like that image. Back to the cars. Hmmmooozzz, they really did look like bees coming in.

More cars had now filled the lot. Penni was a little surprised she was still the only one there. Lazy bastards. Where was everyone. She hitched herself up further on the concrete surrounding the tree and sat Indian style. God, where was everyone. What if she sat here from dawn to dusk without anyone's coming. What a downer.

But then she saw one of the other "mall kids" walking past the car closest to the tree. He eased up beside her.

"You the only one here?" he asked.

It was a stupid question, he could see that she was. "Yah," she said gazing off at the building, "Guess the other bastards are all sleeping off last night's hootch."

He settled against the concrete tree holder and began staring across the parking lot too.

As eager as Penni had been to have someone come, she really had nothing to say. It was now as it usually was—the beginning of the gathering of the kids at the mall.

In the distance Penni saw the groups of shoppers that had been standing by the mall doors begin filing into the mall. It was open. Too early to go in though. She guessed she'd stay out under the tree a while longer. She glanced sideways at her companion. She wondered if he'd had a drink this morning too. He drank, she knew. But she didn't think he liked it as much as she did.

Penni had had her first drink at age five when her real

Dad, who was still living with them then, had given her a sip of beer. She remembered thinking that it tasted very queerly. Her mom didn't drink and didn't like her father's drinking that much. That may have been one of the reasons they eventually got a divorce. They fought over so many things it was hard to tell.

Often children have their first drinks at home—either sips of wine or beer given to them by their parents. Manufacturers have encouraged "transitional drinking"—that is going from soft drinks to alcoholic ones by the distribution of 3.2-beer, "pop" wines, light beer. Indeed many adults believe beer and wine contain less alcohol than hard liquor and therefore are more appropriate to give children. However, in reality one twelve ounce bottle of beer and one four ounce glass of wine and one drink made with a shot (one ounce) of distilled spirits, all have approximately the same alcohol content (.5 oz). One serving of any of these beverages is a "drink" and should be considered as such even if the wine has a "pop" taste or the beer is "light." Perhaps more important is whether or not young people are introduced to drinking within a social or cultural context that allows them over a time to establish a clear sense of how, when, where, what, and how much to drink.

While Penni's dad was still living with them, she had had opportunities to have more drinks. Penni was shy and hated to be teased. When her dad had people over to talk and drink, as he often did, Penni found she got along better if she fortified herself a little in advance with a drink. Most often it would be out of whatever bottle he had gotten out to serve. Several times he had almost caught her doing it. But then her mom and dad had gotten a divorce. Her mom's new husband—Penni still couldn't think of him as a father even though he'd been living with them for two years—didn't drink. So there was no liquor in the house now and Penni had to get her own. With both her mom and the new father working, drinking without being found out wasn't hard, but getting liquor was forever a problem. Penni sighed. Good lord, recently it seemed like half her energy was going into getting it and the other half enjoying it. There didn't seem to be much room for a whole lot else.

Penni uncrossed her legs. She thought she'd wander into the Mall and see if any other kids were there. She didn't say anything to the guy next to her. She just started off slowly. She knew he'd drift along sooner or later. That was the way with the Mall kids.

4 ◈ Jesse—Into It

Jesse began the final bit of sweeping in the living room. His mother woke up when he started picking up the papers.

"Oh," she said. "I just lay down for a minute. I must'a dozed off. Oh, my back. What this house needs is a couch without all these lumpy cushions."

His mom stretched, sat up, and then began rubbing her face with her hands. "I'm going to get washed up while you finish up in here," she said. "My face feels like it's got an extra layer of something on it." She went back to the bathroom without even seeming to notice that he'd done all the rooms except the living room.

Jesse flicked the final bit of obvious dirt into the dustpan and took the broom and dustpan out to the back porch. The house wasn't perfect but there wasn't any point in really scrubbing because it would just get dirty again. For sure his mother wasn't going to put much energy into keeping it clean. He paused momentarily. Maybe he should tell his mother he was going. Then he thought: why bother.

He swung off the porch and went out between the houses and onto the sidewalk. Some kids had scrawled dirty pictures and words on the sidewalk. Jesse remembered when he'd gone through that phase. Before you did "it," it was such big stuff. After you did "it," it was big stuff too but in a different way. He thought of Carolyn, the girl he'd done it with. He didn't like her much then and still didn't. However, if she'd do it again, he'd be willing to pretend he did. Then he shrugged. But that was fantasy. That had happened months ago. The way Carolyn was, she was probably getting paid for it now. There wasn't any way Carolyn was going to be anybody.

Jesse kicked an empty beer bottle, glancing back to see it spin crazily. He was glad it hadn't broken. He liked to see them skitter and spin. He wondered if he would ever be somebody. Jesse was pretty good in school and he worked at it. But there didn't seem to be much connection between what he was learning and anything he saw to be or do. He didn't want to be like Jake and hawk jewelry out of sidewalk trays downtown. He didn't want to be like Ollie and sit behind the counter of a small store each day selling to people who didn't have enough money to pay for what they got. And he certainly didn't want to be like Edgar who picked up trash in the tunnels all day. He wanted to be somebody else. But he wasn't sure who and he didn't have the foggiest idea of how he could get to be it.

Jesse passed a few isolated stores. He wanted to get to where the grocery store was. It wasn't much of a grocery store. It was small and the foodstuffs were piled all over. If you were fat, you really had to be careful walking down the narrow aisles or you'd go knocking cans and bottles off the shelves. Jesse stepped inside. Ollie was busy with a customer. Jesse looked around at the back by the door to the storage area. Sometimes Ollie kept a cardboard box there with boxes that had been opened, cans that had been dented, or items too old to sell on the shelves. He didn't find the box so he started down between the shelves. Finally he found what he was looking for—a package that had been damaged. He picked it up: oyster crackers. He'd never had them but it was better than noodles or something that had to be cooked. He took it up to the counter.

"Look Ollie, this box is all banged up—looks like some of the crackers might even have already spilled out. What do you want for it?"

Ollie pulled the strings on his white grocer's apron to make it tighter and then reached for the box. He examined it and said, "Ten cents off the marked price."

"Look Ollie," Jesse said, "there's probably even crackers already out of it—I don't know how many. How about fifty cents off?"

"It doesn't look that bad to me," Ollie said. "Twenty-five cents off."

"What about thirty-five cents off?"

"Twenty-five cents off," said Ollie.

Jesse wavered. That still made it a bit much. He reached in his pocket and felt the coins. He counted them without taking them out. His fingers knew by shape and by size just what he had. "Twenty-seven cents off. Honest, Ollie, that's all I got."

Ollie looked, sighed. "No wonder I'm still in this store. I'm a lousy business man. OK. Twenty-seven cents off."

Jesse took out his money and laid it on the counter. Ollie picked it up and put it in the cash register without even counting. Jesse didn't understand that. Jesse knew Ollie could trust him. But he also knew it didn't matter. Even if it was your own mother, you counted. Trust didn't do you much good in a world where everybody needed everything they had and more too.

Jesse went outside the store. He had the box open even before he sat down on the curb. He hadn't realized how hungry he really was. Then he remembered that he'd only had a part bowl of cereal for breakfast. He dug in and got a handful of crackers and shoved them into his mouth. He could tell by how far down in the box his hand went the first time that very soon he wasn't going to have any left unless he slowed down. And more than he needed to get full, he needed to make it last. There was only one thing worse than eating all you had and still being hungry, and that was eating all you had *fast* and still being hungry.

Jesse picked out one of the little crackers and looked at it. It had six sides and was puffy. It had been knocked about in the box in such a way its front was broken and Jesse could see inside. The inside was empty. "Rotten cheaters," he said. Selling you a box full of crackers and the crackers full of air. You couldn't trust anybody these days; not even people who made crackers. He put another cracker on end between his front teeth and bit down slowly. The cracker split in half and he had two pieces in his mouth. That was fun. He rolled the cracker to different sides of his mouth. Two crackers for the price of one. He nodded approvingly. Now that was a bargain. He carefully picked out another cracker and put it between his teeth and split it down in two.

Jesse continued to split the crackers in his teeth before eating them. It slowed down the eating process quite a bit and was fun to do. However, long before he reached the last one, he was aware that the crackers had one thing wrong with them. They made you thirsty, damn thirsty. He looked at the one in his hand. Maybe those white bumps on the crackers were salt. The crackers made him thirsty enough for it to be. Damn! He didn't have to reach in his pocket to know that there wasn't any money in there. He needed something to drink.

Jesse finished off the last couple crackers. It didn't matter now that they were not enough to fill him, he needed something to drink. Ollie was busy with customers and wasn't about to go get water for him. Besides Ollie had made it plain years ago: he wasn't no restaurant or park. Damn, thought Jesse. He didn't want to go all the way back home. Plus if he went home he might run into his mom again and he liked the way he had left it, just fine. She'd go out later, but for sure she was still there now.

Jesse got up and started down the street. Maybe in a couple of blocks he'd come up with something. He looked at the overstuffed trash basket on the corner. It had garbage all the way out of it. Bags with their seams all busted out by wet and grease were sitting on the sidewalk next to it. There wasn't any place to put his cracker box. He tossed it in the direction of the trash basket. If they didn't pick up the trash or put out bigger containers, what'd they expect.

"Hey Jesse," a voice from across the street called to him. He looked over. Sitting on the bottom step of an old house were a couple of guys, one of whom he sorta knew from school. The other two he'd seen in the neighborhood. Not all guys stayed in school till the end. The two probably would have been in his grade or a year or two ahead if they'd stayed.

Jesse crossed over. As he neared, he saw that one had a paper bag held by the neck in his hand and the two others were just leaning back smoking. The smell of the smoke told him they weren't regular cigarettes.

"Hey, want some?" said one guy.

Marijuana or "grass" contains a chemical, delta-9-tetra hydrocannabinol (THC), which causes mood and perception changes. This drug, made from the hemp (cannabis) plant has many side effects which are not fully understood at this time. Recreational use of the substance is questionable from a health standpoint and is currently illegal. Health officials are particularly concerned about its use by young people who have not completed physiological and psychological growth. Daily smoking of the drug does lead to lung damage and there is evidence to suspect that the immune system, cellular metabolism, genetic transmission, and the endocrine system are altered in some way by heavy marijuana use. Although adolescence is a time of stress and strain for many young people, psychologists believe these feelings are necessary in learning to cope in the world as an adult. Thus continued "escape" from anxiety and other feelings of adolescence through marijuana use can delay or inhibit transition to adulthood.

"No thanks." Jesse didn't go for pot. To be honest it made him sick. He didn't smoke, and if you didn't smoke, it made it hard to indulge.

"Well, then, have some of this," said the other boy holding out the paper bag. Jesse didn't drink either, but he hesitated.

The other boy saw his hesitation. "C'mon Jesse, I ain't

asking nothing. It's good for you. Makes you a man." He wiggled his pelvis as he said that.

Jesse glanced at the other boys. They were grinning. Jesse still hesitated. He really hated the taste of the stuff and the smell was obnoxious. It was the same smell that often clung to his mother's breath. He didn't much like putting his mouth where the other boys had put theirs either. They were a pretty filthy lot.

"Jesse, c'mon. I ain't gonna sit like an ass with my arm hanging out all day."

Jesse was dying of thirst. "OK," he said and reached for the bag. He was so thirsty he gulped down several swallows before he began to taste it. The taste was certainly foul enough. He had no idea of what he was drinking. He pulled the bottle and bag from his lips and looked down into it. A warm almost burning sensation was spreading through his insides. He glanced at the boy who had given it to him.

"Go ahead," said the other guy gazing at him. "Have one more at it, if you want. I ain't never seen you drink before so I'm enjoying this."

Jesse was still a bit thirsty so he took two more swallows. Then the taste welled up again. It was really disgusting. He handed the bottle and the bag back. The warm feeling was still there and spreading.

Ethyl alcohol (ethanol) is a colorless inflammable liquid formed by fermentation. When drunk in beverages it has an intoxicating or anesthetic effect. Beer and wine are both products of a natural fermentation process. Grains and grapes are exposed to yeasts which convert the vegetable sugars into alcohol. After the alcohol level reaches about fourteen percent, the yeasts die from exposure to their own creation. Distilled spirits (liquors such as Scotch, bourbon, gin, vodka, rum, rye) are made by boiling fermented brews of various types until the alcohol (which boils sooner than the other liquids) is separated as it is turned into steam. Then it is captured and turned to liquid again in a cooling tube. Alcohol is a food in that it contains calories (210 calories per ounce of pure alcohol) but they are "empty calories" because they contain little or no nutritional value. Therefore when a person consumes a great number of calories in alcohol, malnutrition can be a problem.

"All right." "That's the way," said the other two. Just then a car careened down the street. Some guys were hanging out. One boy was beating the side with his hand and all were yelling. As the car passed, one boy on the passenger's side leaned way out the window and gave them a sign. Then the car passed and swerved around the corner.

The boys on the steps stared after it. "Shit," said one. "Those bastards think they just so smart."

"That was Chunky at the wheel, I seen it, but I don't know whose car it was," said another.

"Just once I'd like to have a car and go run by them," said the first boy. Then he added, "Or run over them."

They grinned at that.

"Oh hell," said the second. "If we had a car, I'd do that too."

"Not me," finally said the third boy. "I'd be up there at Trixie D's getting me a couple of ladies to accompany me on a midnight ride."

They all grinned at his idea.

"Hey, here comes Davey."

"Davey boy, over here," they called as another boy approached. "What you got, my man," they asked.

"What you got?" Davey replied.

"Well, probably a little something better than you got," they answered.

"You are right," Davey said. "But, I will share what I've got if you will share what you've got." With that Davey unzipped the lightweight rain jacket he was wearing and produced an extra tall can of beer. Jesse could see that it had been opened but that a piece of foil had been stuffed in the top to keep it from spilling.

"That all you got?" one of the boys asked.

"Yes," said Davey. "But it's all yours. I've had a couple before this one." With that he passed it to the boy with the bottle who handed him his bag as he took it. Each took a swallow or two from the can and passed it on. Then it was handed to Jesse.

Jesse was feeling very mellow and friendly at this time. It didn't seem right not to accept the friendship being offered. He raised the can to his lips. He'd had beer before. This tasted good after the yicky hard stuff. He took several swallows. By this time the first boy had his bag back and was drinking from it and the others were exchanging drags on a roach. Jesse felt awkward standing with the can. He could tell it was light enough just to have one or two swallows left. He raised the can to his lips and finished it off. Then he tossed it down beside the steps where other trash and dirt had accumulated. He felt more warmth spread throughout his insides.

People feel warm inside while drinking because alcohol has a direct irritating effect on the mouth, esophagus, and stomach. There is a barrier in the stomach which prevents the stomach's acidic secretions from causing the stomach to digest itself. Heavy alcohol intake can cause the stomach to become inflamed and this condition is termed "erosive gastritis." Over time alcohol breaks down the stomach's natural barrier and ulcers may develop. Aspirin should be avoided by those drinking excessively because it speeds up the erosive process.

Jesse looked at the other boys. These guys were O.K. he decided. One cracked a joke and he laughed really hard with them. It almost didn't matter what they said, he enjoyed it and found it funny. Jesse had no idea of how much time passed as they joked and talked. Finally, however, the group was out of everything. The bottle had been finished and with the bag sent to follow the beer can. The joints had been smoked. The group began to separate. First one boy, then another ambled off.

"Wanna come on with me?" the boy who had had the bottle finally asked Jesse.

Jesse—Into It 27

"No thanks," mumbled Jesse. "Some other time. I got stuff hanging." Jesse had no idea where the boy was going but his body told him he wasn't up to much more of anything. He started off toward home.

As Jesse walked, he realized the street lights had been turned on. He looked at them and found they got fat and then thin as he walked. He went by Ollie's store. Ollie was inside sweeping. The cans in the window formed a wonderful pattern but Jesse couldn't read the labels. Ollie's hand appeared to wave at him and dimly he heard Ollie call out a greeting. But the words didn't seem to reach him in a way that he could hear and respond to. He kept moving on. Now he had to concentrate on his walking to keep his feet going right.

Only twenty percent of alcohol swallowed is absorbed in the stomach. Eighty percent enters the bloodstream through the small intestine. The blood alcohol concentration (BAC) is used in most states to determine whether or not a person is legally drunk. Once in the bloodstream, because it is soluble in water, the alcohol is able to pass through cell walls and reach all body tissues. Thus a breath test can determine the amount of alcohol in the bloodstream. As alcohol is carried by the bloodstream to the brain and other parts of the nervous system, normal reactions and functions are affected. The greater the BAC the slower the brain functioning. Sensory responses (such as sight, touch, taste, smell, hearing) and motor responses (such as leg movement, arm movement) are dependent on normal brain function and thus are directly affected.

God, I feel funny, Jesse thought. I didn't have that much. But yet all of a sudden.... Jesse felt a rush of sickness in his stomach. Oh, God, he thought, I feel awful. He tried to hurry on. I've got to get home. But the sickness started to churn. His whole body felt like it was turning. His feet couldn't steer his body correctly. It was so hot out, if only he could get in front of a fan.

Then he felt everything in his stomach come up and pour out of his mouth. It went down his pant leg and over his shoe. He tried to pull his foot back but when he did, it was too late. He stood with his legs apart, bending over, as he gagged and threw up again. His head was pounding. His heart was pounding. His eyes were opened wide as the heaving began again. He threw up once more. The taste and smell overwhelmed him. He had no idea how far he had gotten toward home.

Mother, he thought, I can't stand this. Help me. He retched again. This time less came up. Maybe I'll stop now, he thought. But he retched again. Suddenly he felt very weak. He retched again. Almost nothing came out now. He gagged and tried to spit but there didn't seem to be anything there. He felt he couldn't stand up anymore. He moved forward a step or two to get away from the spot where he had just thrown up. The he sank down on his hands and knees. With his head hanging he continued to heave. He had heard of the "dry" heaves but had never before had them.

Oh God, why did he keep throwing up when there was no more to come out. He closed his eyes. Bright shoots of lights appeared as he gagged and heaved. They looked like the footprints of a chicken. "Chicken tracks," he murmured incoherently, "Chicken tracks, chicken tracks."

Throwing up after too much drinking is the body's reaction to the irritating effects of alcohol. Repeated vomiting episodes, as a result of long term drinking, can lead to death if the esophagus is ruptured or if bleeding from esophageal veins that have become distended or weak occurs.

After what seemed an endless amount of time, Jesse's heaves gradually subsided. He was weak and exhausted. He continued motionless on his hands and knees until he felt as if he had enough strength to move. The skin on his hands was all marbled from the rough sidewalk. He felt the hurt from his knees where they were being pressed against the sidewalk cement. He lifted his knee and tried to steady his hand on it in an effort to raise himself. His hand slipped. There was squishy vomit all over his pant leg and the wet was beginning to soak through to his skin. "Ohhhh," he found himself moaning out loud. He got up unsteadily and forced himself to walk toward home. His heart was still racing and he wondered if he would make it. He hoped his mother wasn't home to see him. He couldn't stand trying to talk to her, explain. He just needed to get to his bed.

When Jesse got to the house, he saw the lights were out. He went around to the back and pulled himself up onto the back porch by the banister. He walked into the house bent over. He knew he needed a bath. He didn't want to lie down with the vomit on. But he just didn't have the strength to take one. He somehow managed to get out of his clothes. He knew he still had bits of vomit clinging to him but he couldn't do anything about it. He wiped his hand off as best he could with his shorts.

Jesse sank down onto his bed. Oh, God, he had never felt so terrible. Would he ever feel human again? He had no idea when sleep came but soon he lapsed into a deep unknowing.

5 ❧ Christine—Into It

Christine walked slowly across her room. She flipped the pages of a book on her nightstand and then started back to her dressing room table. She had on her best lacey underclothes. She didn't want to put her dress on too soon. She was ready far too early but then, she had started three hours ahead of time.

Christine still couldn't believe it—tonight she was going to the Danvers' party just like Sandra! Her insides fluttered a little as she thought about it. But it was true. Sandra had called in the middle of the week saying some boy from Kentucky, part of the horsie set there, was here showing horses at the Southeastern Charity Show. And he was a friend of Mark Geigy's family and somehow they had gotten this guy invited to the Danvers' party too. The girl Mark wanted this guy to take couldn't come and so Mark had asked Sandra to get someone and she had called Christine. Ordinarily Christine would have been miffed at being second choice. But good lord, Mark Geigy didn't even know she existed. Sandra could have picked anyone. Sandra was a super friend to have chosen Christine!

Then Christine had had to convince her mom and dad to

let her go. Her dad was really no problem: "If this boy is a friend of Matt Geigy's son, then I am sure he is a fine boy," was her father's only response.

Christine had decided not to really ask her parents whether or not she could go: that might create problems—what if her parents said "no." Christine decided to inform them she was going in as casual a manner as possible. She thought about it the whole morning before she did it. Everyone was always just informing everyone else in the house what they were doing. And generally when she did go on dates—to the basketball game or to the movies, she just told them where she was going, who she was going with, and when she'd be in.

Christine waited until just before bedtime. Her father had not been home for dinner so it really wasn't possible then. She didn't want to tell her mother alone for fear she'd ask questions and start thinking. Some secret sense told Christine that if her mother thoroughly understood that Christine wanted to go to an adult party where there would be drinking (and go with an older boy she didn't even know!) she wouldn't let her go.

Christine had taken a bath that night and then come down to say good night. "The swim coach says we are going to practice tomorrow afternoon since we missed Tuesday's practice because of rain. He thinks we've got a good chance of beating Oak Hills in Sunday afternoon's match," Christine opened. "So I'll be at the club till almost dinner time but I'm going to get a ride home."

"That's fine, dear," mumbled her mother. She had the membership lists spread all over the couch and was checking something about them. Her father was reading the paper.

"And Saturday Sandra and I are double dating," Christine wanted to stop there but she thought she better add just a little more. "She's going with Mark Geigy and I'm going with an out-of-town friend of his."

"Mark Geigy?" Her mother looked up a bit puzzled. "He's not in your class, is he dear?"

Christine didn't answer immediately.

Her father looked up from his paper. "What's the difference, Kathy?" he said. "I'm sure any friend of Matt Geigy's son is a fine boy."

"Well, I suppose it's OK," Christine's mother glanced back at her membership lists.

"And the dance teacher wants us to begin selecting our costumes for the fall recital. Do you want to make mine this year or should I have her order one? She says if we order, we really ought to order two months in advance. They come from New York. Last year, remember, she ordered them a month in advance and we didn't get them in time for dress rehearsal." Christine had purposely saved that announcement hoping to distract her mother. It worked. The thought of making Christine's dance costume completely took over her mother's mind and she appeared to forget about the date.

"Well, Christine, you know how hard it is to get materials to match if some of the girls order them and some try to make them. I would say if most of them are going to order them, you order too." She paused. "It was different when I was a girl, my mother always made mine; so did the other mothers. But today things are so different. With so many of the mothers working, they just don't care about their daughters the way our mothers did about us."

Christine was aware her mother seemed to have something against mothers who worked. She never seemed to pass up an opportunity to make a remark about it. Christine was not sure why. For example, Kay's mother worked. She was a real estate person and sold homes. Whenever Christine saw her she looked busy and happy. And she seemed to have enough time for Kay. Of course she worked crazy hours. When people came into town and had just a few days to choose a home before they moved here, Kay's mother spent endless hours with those people and she really couldn't take time for anything else. Christine wasn't sure whether or not Kay's mother had to work. But she seemed to like it so much Christine had the feeling she would be doing it regardless. Christine didn't want to be like her own mother and do nothing when she grew up. She couldn't imagine selling real estate either. She didn't know what she wanted to be. Anyway, at least she had gotten an OK of sorts for the party.

Part of the process of changing from a child into an adult is developing a sense of personal identity separate from one's parents. Another part of the process is selecting a means of supporting oneself in the future. At one time parents chose careers for their children by apprenticing them into various trades. Today's youth have many more opportunities than in the past. Increased educational opportunities mean that they can prepare themselves for a wide variety of occupations. For both young men and young women, however, role models are important. Realistically it is difficult to aspire to something one knows nothing about. Therefore youth constantly appraise their environment and the people they know in an effort to develop a clearer sense of direction for themselves.

Christine's thoughts were interrupted by her mother's voice.

"Well, dear, I see you're almost ready." Her mother walked over to Christine's mirror and began touching her own hair. "What time did you say this boy is coming?"

"About eight."

"Well, then, you'll be ready in plenty of time." She turned to face Christine. "Where did you you say you were going again?"

"To a party," Christine answered. She busied herself straightening her bed, hoping her mother wouldn't ask any more.

Her mother turned back to the mirror. "Where's the party being held?"

Christine kept busy at her bed. A lump came into her throat. "The Danvers," she said as casually as she could.

"The Danvers!" Her mother's hand fell to her side. Even though Christine couldn't see her, she could feel her mother turning to look at her. "Well, I thought their boys were all in college. I didn't think they had youngsters any more."

Christine just shrugged.

"That's a rather grown up party," her mother said taking a few steps toward Christine. "I don't really know as I want you. . . ."

Christine turned quickly. "Mother, I don't know that we're going there for the whole evening but this boy did have his horse in the show and I suspect going for a while is, well, you know, like a social obligation or something. We'll probably just go on from there. What's the matter, don't you trust me?"

"Well, of course, I trust you, Christine. But the Danvers' boys are part of a much older group." (And Christine could hear her mother thinking "and a much rougher group." There were always rumors about the Danvers' boys being rather a fast crowd.)

"My goodness, it's their parents' party," said Christine.

"But I mean they'll probably not have special arrangements for the children."

"Mother!" said Christine. "I am not a child anymore."

"No dear," her mother hastened, "I didn't mean to say you were. I just meant, well, you don't drink or smoke or do anything of the things that older people do at parties and I. . . ."

Christine interrupted again. "But I do think, I do talk, and I can dance, and those are things older people do at parties. Look, mom, I'm almost all ready to go. They'll be here very soon. Let's not start up, huh? I'll be OK."

"Well, dear," her mother said. "I suppose it is too late to do much of anything. I just wish I'd known. Did you tell me all this before?"

"All what before, mom?" Christine said. "I told you last Wednesday I was going to a party with the friend of Mark Geigy and Sandra."

"I know, dear, but did you mention the Danvers?"

"Oh mom, I don't remember exactly what I said, but nobody said anything then so why should they now?"

One of the ways people learn is by doing. It may not be the experience itself that teaches so much as the individual's reflection on the experience and what he or she learns from that process. Parents and young people are often in conflict regarding what constitutes appropriate experiences for age and maturity levels. Parents fear young people will find themselves in situations they can't handle or are negative. Young people want to reach out, explore, learn. Parents can ease the situation by continually helping young people prepare for new experiences so that young people can take greater advantage of them when they do occur and parents can have more confidence in their child's ability to deal with them.

Christine walked around to the other side of the bed to where she had laid out her dress and picked it up. She would have liked to have gotten a new one like Sandra had, but she was afraid her mother would have gotten suspicious and started asking more about the party. She began putting it on, hoping once her head was inside it might drown out any additional comments her mother made.

"My goodness, I'd forgotten about that dress," her mother said. "You don't think it's a little too fallish, dear?"

Christine's head popped out. "No mom, I think it will do just fine." Actually, it was a little fallish. But on the other hand, it was the most grown-up of all her dresses and she couldn't imagine going to the Danvers' party in school-girl summer frills.

Christine needed to get her mother out of the room. She was starting to bug her. Also Christine needed time to fix her hair a new way. She couldn't do it until she had her dress on and she needed to get started. She groped for words. "Mom, be a love and check to see the outside lights are on. Sandra knows which our house is but I want it to look lit up and pretty when they come."

That was a request her mother understood. Whenever her father's guests came, her mother flitted around endlessly beforehand, turning up this light, turning down that light (they had dimmer switches everywhere) "to make the house have that lived in, yet elegant look" her mother used to say.

"All right, dear," her mother said. She walked over and straightened the strap on Christine's dress and then started out the door. She paused long enough to say. "You'll be home early, won't you?"

"I'm not sure, mom," Christine said, "but I'll be sure to call if I know we are going to be late."

Christine's mother nodded almost absently and went on downstairs, the thick carpeting almost immediately hiding the sound of her footsteps.

Christine quickly sat down at the mirror. She had had a lot of time before, but now she was going to be a bit pushed. She wanted to wear her hair up with some side curls. She'd seen that style in a movie magazine and thought it was sexy. But she needed a bit of time to work it out.

Christine was putting the last pin in her hair as the doorbell rang. Her heart skipped a beat. They're here. She took one final look in the mirror. She liked what she saw. Sandra had said her new dress made her look at least two years older. "Well, Christine," Christine said to herself, "I think your hairdo makes you look at least two years older." She leaned toward the mirror examining her make-up one last time. "Well, here goes, Cinderella," she said. Christine turned out the light and went downstairs.

A half hour later, Christine walked with her escort, whose name was Arthur, into the den of the big Danvers' house. There was a crowd around the bar that had been set up there. Christine knew from other reports that there were probably three or four more bars set up elsewhere in the house.

"Excuse me," her date said beginning to move toward the bar, "I'll be right back, bourbon and ginger OK?"

Christine nodded. She completely forgot what she was going to say. She had been practicing things like "Make mine gin and tonic but leave out the gin. I've had my quota this week." But somehow she forgot when the time came. Well, she could always just stand and hold her drink pretending to sip. That was probably a better thing to do anyway. She looked around. Everyone here was definitely older. She'd fit in more if she had a drink in her hand.

Many people simply do not know how to say "no" when offered a drink. Refusing skills can be very important and are worth practicing. Young people might practice them with a friend or parent. "No thanks" is usually sufficient. However, in some cases one may have to say, "No thank you, if I want some I will ask for it." The extreme is leaving a situation in which one is put under so much pressure, it is uncomfortable to be there.

It is so common in our society to accept food and drinks as a polite gesture of friendship, people often feel guilty when they refuse. Yet it is clear each individual has a right to decide what he does or does not want to take into his system. A California group (Nondrinkers' Rights, Concord, California) has developed a six-point "bill of rights" for nondrinkers.

1. *Nondrinkers have the right to refuse a drink without being considered a social deviate.*
2. *Nondrinkers have the right to the availability of nonalcoholic beverages at parties, lounges, social and recreational functions.*
3. *Nondrinkers have the right to fair and equitable governmental consideration as is afforded other minority groups.*
4. *Nondrinkers have the right not to be subjected to overt and subliminal liquor advertisements.*
5. *Nondrinkers have the right to be heard at the level of press, radio and TV.*
6. *Nondrinkers have the right not to be subjected to the hazards created by the drinker—on the highways, in the home, and in the community.*

Christine felt very awkward standing by herself. She was grateful when she saw Arthur returning.

He handed her her drink. "Let's move out of here, it's getting crowded."

They moved past people and down the hall into a bigger room. The room had french doors leading out to a veranda which was gaily lit. There seemed to be people everywhere.

"Taste your drink," Arthur said. "I told them not to make it very strong. We might be in for a long evening of drinking. Also I wanted to talk to you rather than getting soused right away."

Somehow the way Arthur put things was reassuring to Christine. Christine obediently sipped her drink. The ginger ale was there all right but a tingling taste was added. She had expected to hate it but it wasn't bad.

Arthur took a sip of his. "What I really like is good old sippin' bourbon—you wouldn't dare contaminate it with stuff with this. But nobody uses that for a set-up bar."

Christine nodded. She wasn't exactly sure what sippin' bourbon was but she got the gist that it must be a better quality bourbon than she was having in her drink. Arthur must know a lot about drinking. She took another sip.

Various words are used to describe the taste of alcoholic drinks: smooth, rich, full-bodied, mellow, dry, light, charcoal, and so forth. More important is the amount of alcohol in the drink. Beer averages four percent alcoholic content, while most table wines are approximately twelve percent alcoholic content. The strength of ethyl alcohol in distilled spirits (liquors) is indicated by the term "proof." One hundred proof means half the content (fifty percent) of the beverage is ethyl alcohol. Eighty proof means forty percent of the beverage is ethyl alcohol. Liquor bottles are labeled as to "proof." By dividing the "proof" by two, the alcoholic content of the beverage can be determined. In general, it's wise to know the alcoholic content of drinks as a guide to consumption. If the drink has a low concentration of alcohol, one takes in less alcohol with each sip. "Social drinking" ends when intoxication begins.

Christine—Into It

Since neither Christine nor Arthur knew anyone but Sandra and Mark who had disappeared the minute they had gotten inside the door, it left them on their own.

"Want to explore?" said Arthur. "I've never been here before. I'd like to see what it's like."

Christine took another sip of her drink and then took Arthur's outstretched hand as he led her into the next room. Christine didn't know what she had expected the Danvers' house to look like. It wasn't a mansion. Actually it was a lot plainer than she had thought it would be, given all their money. They obviously weren't interested in antiques. But, in a way, that was what she expected of the horsies. Someone had once told her, they always put more money in their barns than they did their houses. She knew white board fence like they had around many of their horse fields was expensive so it was probably true.

Much of the conversation as she passed by seemed to be about horses: "Gelding. . . ." "Over fifteen hands high. . . ." "Equestrian competition. . . ." The phrases floated past her ears until she felt like they were walking around in a tapestry of horse talk. Twice someone stopped Arthur and congratulated him on his ride. On the way to the party, Christine had found out Arthur had gotten a "Third" in the Morgan Pleasure Horse competition. She was grateful, however, he didn't insist on talking about horses. Christine was taking horseback riding lessons for the fun of it this summer but she didn't know anything about horses—breeding, bloodlines, composition points, special gates like the "rack"—all those things horsey people were interested in. All she knew was that it was fun to get up on an animal and learn to make it do what you wanted it to. And that some horses seemed easier to ride than others.

Christine heard music in the distance. "Where's that coming from?" she questioned Arthur.

"Let's find out." They went out the sunroom door and followed a path down to the small lake area not far from the house. Under a pink and white striped tent cover, a portable dance floor had been put down and there was a band playing.

"Want to?" Arthur asked.

"Sure," said Christine. They set their drink glasses down by the outside bar.

Christine was delighted to find Arthur was a good dancer and they stayed on the floor for about five different pieces. When the band switched to one of those slow dreamy tunes older people liked, however, they decided to quit.

"Whew, that was great," said Arthur. "But I'm thirsty. Be back in a second."

Christine watched him go up to the bar and return with two more drinks. She had thought of telling him to leave out the bourbon but then she changed her mind. She was thirsty and they did taste good. Christine felt her earlier tension go. She was starting to have a super time. Arthur was really a very nice date. It didn't seem to bother him that Mark was still nowhere in sight. Christine had thought she might see Sandra and Mark on the dance floor, but then again, there were lots of people and many different places to go.

The band seemed temporarily stuck on the slow ones. "Want to explore some more?" Arthur asked.

Christine nodded.

"Take another sip so we can carry these along with us. The bartender made them a little full."

Christine obediently sipped.

There were little yellow light bulbs strung along through the trees lining the pathways. Some people were strolling down to the barns while others were returning to the house. Some were making their way down to the band area.

"Where do you want to go?" Arthur asked.

"Let's see the rest of the house," Christine said. They walked back up the walk. Christine had seen a number of people going down the stairs off the main hallway. "I want to see what's on the lower level," she said.

When they got in the house though, she first excused herself and made her way to the ladies' powder room upstairs. She set her drink on the dressing table in the powder room,

Christine—Into It

went to the john, fixed her make-up and was ready to go again. She looked down at her drink. This would be a perfect place to ditch it or forget it. She hesitated. The only other woman in the powder room left. Christine picked up the glass and posed in front of the mirror. First she held the drink casually to her lips, her elbow resting daintily in the other hand. Then she held the drink in both hands about waist high and turned sideways. She liked her image with the drink. She did look quite sophisticated and worldly, she thought. Besides it tasted OK. And Arthur had said he had asked the bartender to make them "light." She didn't think she would know the difference between light and heavy but it probably was light.

Drinking is viewed as adult behavior in our society. We have laws in each state to mark the legal drinking age. In recent years, there has been a great confusion among the public as to what the legal drinking age should be. Some states have lowered the drinking age from twenty-one to eighteen and others have gone back and forth. There is nothing magic about an eighteenth or twenty-first birthday in regard to maturity and drinking. Maturity about drinking implies conscious decision-making about oneself and drinking based on knowledge of self and the properties of alcohol. However, it is clear that heavy drinking during adolescence can stunt overall development and impair the total maturation of the personality—so many strong arguments can be made about the benefits to young people of not drinking at all until at least the legal age limit has been reached.

Arthur was waiting for her at the bottom of the staircase. They went on downstairs. There was an enormous den in the basement. This was obviously where the Danvers did a lot of their entertaining. A formal built-in bar graced one end of the room. There were several small tables with low chairs. Christine had noted that upstairs, maids passed trays of small sandwiches to eat, and hired bartenders served drinks. Down here things were set out more casually. There were bowls of nuts on the tables. Christine also noticed the man behind the bar was not a regular bartender. He was grayed and quite distinguished looking. He had on a plaid sport jacket. That might even be Mr. Danvers, Christine thought. Who else would it be? But then why would he tend bar at his own parties? The man poured someone a drink and then continued what seemed to be an earnest conversation with two couples perched at the bar.

Christine and Arthur sank down on a leather covered couch for two. Arthur put his arm around her shoulder and she nestled down so her head rested lightly against his arm. They sat sipping their drinks, commenting on the people and the room. It was dimly lit in the den and there was quite a bit of smoke. Christine found herself feeling more and more relaxed and less and less self-conscious. She loved the fact that no one paid any attention to them. It was sort of a do-it-yourself party.

Occasionally over-raucous laughter came from some of the tables. And some of the language was rough. It wasn't that Christine had never heard it before: it was just that it was so loud and open. Arthur was very attentive. He left her side only to get them another drink. The man at the bar was so engrossed in his conversation, he filled Arthur's order without stopping to talk to him.

"Still don't know who he is," said Arthur as he sat back down an put his arm around her. They grinned at one another.

Christine couldn't believe she could be so comfortable with someone she had met only a few hours before. They sipped their drinks.

"You know, I really like you," Arthur said. Christine looked up at Arthur. He leaned down and kissed her very fully and deliberately. She was a bit surprised and yet it seemed liked the natural thing to do. Nobody seemed to notice. After he had gently removed his lips from hers, Christine slowly raised her glass and took another drink. She was surprised to find she had finished it.

Christine—Into It

What people learn about that which is and is not acceptable in human relationships is stored in the cerebral cortex of the brain. The depressant action of alcohol on the brain cells causes a temporary lapse in normal functioning. Thus people act more on feeling levels than on learned behavior levels after they have been drinking. People enjoy "loosening up" by drinking. They relax and don't worry so much about what they may do or say. Drinking can become a problem, however, if the person drinks to the point that his or her behavior goes way beyond the bounds of what is considered socially acceptable.

Christine sat contentedly. She really would have liked another drink but she didn't want Arthur to leave to get it. They had stopped talking and were staring dreamily out into the smoke.

"There you two are!" A voice broke in on Christine's thoughts. "We've been looking all over for you. It's late and my parents are going to have fits if I don't get home," said Sandra.

"Why? What time is it?" asked Christine.

"Quarter to two."

"Quarter to two!" Christine sat up startled. "Are you sure?"

"Sure I'm sure."

Christine could not imagine how it had gotten to be that hour. It seemed like they'd just been at the party a short time. "Oh, golly, I told mom I'd call if I was going to be late. I'm sure they expected me about 12:30."

"Let's go," said Sandra.

"Maybe I better call," Christine said.

"Let's not take the time," Sandra said.

"No, I better call." Christine insisted. "It won't take long. I saw a phone in a bedroom when I went to the john." She hurried upstairs.

Later that evening, Christine climbed slowly into bed. There was so much filling her head it was hard to concentrate on any one thing. She had had a wonderful time. Even though her parents were upset about her getting home so late, the fact that finally she had called had helped. Her head danced with memories of Arthur, the bobbing lights in the trees, the dancing, the quiet time on the couch, his kiss at the party and his good night kiss. She smiled in contentment and turned on her side to go to sleep.

All of a sudden the room started to swim. Then it started to go round. She turned over on her back trying to stop it. But it didn't help. Her stomach felt funny. She sat up. That helped a little. Things slowed down. Maybe if I prop my head up on pillows, she thought.

Christine got out of bed shakily and took the pillows off her settee and piled them under her bed pillow. Carefully she lay back down trying not to jar her equilibrium. The room began whirling again. She sat up. Suddenly she felt desperately tired. She wanted to lie down and go to sleep. Her shoulders sagged as she sat in bed. Her head bent forward a little. She felt her stomach tighten as she tried to keep control of it. Maybe if I turn up the air-conditioning she thought. She went out into the hall. The control switch was for the whole house, there was no individual room switch. She'd just have to make it all cooler. She heard the whirr as the air-conditioning unit started and began blowing cold air out through the ventilator system.

Christine made her way back to her room touching the walls for support as she went. She climbed in bed. Again she tried to lie down but the room went around so fast she sat up for fear she might get sick if she didn't. "I'm so tired," she murmured to herself. Her head bent forward. She shut her eyes. The room turned. She kept her eyes closed. Then she felt her head jerk up; she must have dozed. She opened her eyes. Then she closed them again. Oh, if only she could lie down. She was so tired. She felt her head nodding. She dozed and her head jerked up uncomfortably again.

"Oh please, please," she murmured, "I just want to go to sleep."

Finally she decided to lie down on the pile of pillows again. Lying on her back wasn't her usual sleep position but she felt less dizzy than on her side. She tried to close her eyes. The room was going around. If only she could keep her eyes closed and hold on, maybe she could fall asleep. "Hold on," she murmured. "Hold on." Then she was asleep.

When Christine awoke in the morning, she was freezing. The air-conditioner was still going full blast and she had almost no covers on. "Geez, I must have turned it down to zero in here." She started out her door but stopped when she saw her mother in the hall reaching for the air-conditioning control with a puzzled look on her face.

Christine didn't say anything. Instead she put on her bathrobe and slid back under the covers. She had an enormous headache and felt like she needed to crawl back into the healing sleep she'd just crawled out of.

If dizzy sick feelings occur after drinking, finding a quiet environment is helpful. One should be near a bathroom if possible in case there is an urge to vomit. Most people find that the room seems to spin if they lie down. On the other hand, the sooner the person can get to sleep, the better. Never take unprescribed sleeping pills to get to sleep though because they work along with alcohol to further depress the brain and taken in quantity can be life threatening. Drugstore medicine for nausea may help. Support from a friend or family member can also help make the experience more bearable. It takes about one hour for one drink to be metabolized by the liver. It takes about eight hours for all the alcohol to leave the body after it has been metabolized.

6 ⌇ Penni—Into It

As she entered the Mall, Penni made a point of taking the escalator down and going by Rickles first. Rickles was sort of a dime store crossed with a low-class discount house. Penni could never figure out how they got in the Mall. They certainly didn't fit with the class of the other stores. The store front was wide open. They had four big check-out counters almost like those in a grocery store which formed a barrier halfway across the opening. The rest of the space in front was filled with one-way "in" turnstiles. They pulled a big ugly iron gate across the front at night. No other store had anything like it. It was obviously the kind of store that expected shoplifting.

One of Penni's friends, Candy, was just putting her cash drawer in one of the check-out places. The fact that Penni didn't have to go into the store made it easy to step up and talk to Candy.

"Hey, wanna join us tonight?" Penni asked, perching on the end of the check-out counter.

"I don't know," Candy said. "What time are you starting? I don't get off here till six and after being on my feet all day, I'm gonna have to go home and sit down for a while."

Penni—Into It

Candy was older than Penni—you had to be sixteen to get a working permit. Her father had helped her get the job. Most of the time the college kids got the summer jobs not the high schoolers. But Candy's father drove a delivery truck for Rickles. Penni didn't think Candy was a very good cashier. The lines behind her stand were always longer than the others because she was so slow at ringing up. But since she was Penni's friend, Penni tried not to notice.

Penni was pretty sure Candy's Dad had pushed hard for the job because Candy had started hanging out at the Mall so much. Sometimes now Candy went off with the girls who worked behind the counter at the ice cream store or one of the guys who demonstrated toys and put up stock at the toy store. Penni didn't like the fact that now Candy seemed to have more in common with the kids who worked at the Mall than she did with the kids who hung out there.

A few generations ago, most children were working to help support their families at age sixteen. There is an increasingly long gap between the young person and his or her career. This gap has led many young people to feel a deep sense of worthlessness and alienation toward the world of work. These feelings contribute to an atmosphere where alcohol and drug abuse can flourish. Young people need help and encouragement in finding meaningful work—jobs that provide satisfaction and allow significant learning to take place. Many mental health professionals believe that bridging the current gap between school and work should be a priority for our society.

Penni wanted to keep on the good side of Candy because now Candy got paid and that meant sometimes Candy was a "source."

"Hey," said Candy, "here comes my boss. You better beat it. He told me last week, he didn't like me standing around talking with my friends. He said it didn't look good for the store's image."

"But there's nobody here yet!"

"I know, I know. But that doesn't matter to him. So you better move on, OK?"

"Sure," Penni said, sliding off the end of the check-out counter. "See you tonight, OK?" Penni gave a dirty look to the store manager who was moving down the aisles toward the cash register. Since he was looking at the stock as he walked, he didn't see it. Too bad, thought Penni. Next time, I'll give him my double kazoo thumb.

Penni moved off down the Mall. She looked in at the piano and organ store. The lacy metal door that the shopkeeper pulled down at night had been rolled back up in the ceiling and the lights were on but Penni didn't see anyone. Too bad. Off and on, whenever the store was open, someone sat at the small organ in front and played happy-sounding songs. Penni liked to stand and listen. She watched the hands of whoever played, thinking that someday she might be able to learn to do that. However, her mom never seemed interested in having her do much other than go to school.

Research has shown that young people with poor self-images are at risk to abuse alcohol and other drugs. Basically, the person with a low self-esteem will do just about anything to be liked by others. Being known as a "stoner" or "junkie" makes some teenagers feel special.

Everyone has a need to feel special and there are a number of things parents, teachers, and friends of young people can do to promote a positive self-image. The first place to start is to spend time with young people. It is true that quality is more important than quantity but in all close human relationships simply being together is the first step. People feel special when others take time out to be with them. The next step is spending the time doing something which is likely to make each participant feel a sense of joy or accomplishment. Children should be asked how they feel about things, helped to deal with intense emotions, and have their positive characteristics stressed over shortcomings.

Penni reached the Mall center. She stopped surprised. Last week a model car had been revolving there. It had been maroon with gold flecks through the paint and had a futuristic design. The kids had all spent a lot of time looking at it. Penni never saw it being driven either in or out so she secretly thought it probably couldn't even go. Even if it could go, who would want to take it out on the road? Somebody'd just gawk at it and cause it to be smashed up. However, the car was gone and in its place was a small stage and a sign advertising a "Mickey Mouse Revue" at 3:30.

"Mickey Mouse," Penni laughed. The Mall was always having these promotional things to get people in. It would be toddler time in the Mall again this afternoon.

Penni passed by the center section and took the escalator on the other side that went up. She headed back toward the center section on the upper floor and turned to the left. Down the corridor she heard the noise of the pinball machines. Good, some of the Mall kids were already there.

Penni walked down to the third store and stepped in. One of the kids gave her a nod and moved over so she could watch him play his machine. Penni loved the familiar sound of bells ringing, flippers whacking, car motors accelerating, cars crashing, space booms, and other assorted noises. She liked it best when they were all going at once. She watched as the guy next to her pressed his flipper frantically in an effort to get a higher score. Some kids were really addicts at this. She once watched a kid spend fifteen dollars worth of quarters in no time at all just playing the machines.

Penni remembered the Mall before they had put the machines in. The Mall people didn't like the kids hanging around. They felt it made the place look bad. At first they had tried to shoo them off. That didn't work well. Even when the kids did get shooed out they always came back. Then she guessed the management had decided if the kids were going to be there, they might as well try to keep them in one area so they had converted one of the small stores into this pinball place. It was nice. There was a red and silver flashing light in the back. There was carpet on the floor and it was kinda dark. It had about a dozen machines in it. Penni figured they made a lot of money on the place too. Well, not a lot of money but certainly enough that it wasn't a washout.

When he finished his game, the boy turned. "Wanna have

a match game on that one?" The machine was called "Space Wars" and had buttons for two players.

"Naw," said Penni. "I don't have the dough with me today."

"I'll stake you to one game," the boy said pulling two quarters from his pocket as they approached the machine.

Penni moved to one side so he could put the quarter in the slot in front of her. He put one in the slot on his side too. "Ready go," he said.

Penni pushed a button and her space ship appeared on the machine. Another image appeared on the screen too. She took evasive action and fired a rocket. Boom, direct hit! She brought up her second ship and began manuevering after his.

"Ach," she cried. He had just blown up her first ship. She sent another missile up and took evasive action with her second ship. Fire! Boom, she got his missile launcher. Now they were both fighting with their remaining rockets. Fire! Oh, shucks a miss! Damn it, she was almost out of rockets and time. He fired but she had just taken evasive action. He missed. But he had fired two in a row. She pressed down. He missed but barely. She fired with her final rocket. Oh, no! She missed! He wheeled his second rocket. Boom! Her ship exploded on the screen. And then the machine went dead.

The boy smiled. His quarter had been well spent. He had won. However, she knew she had been a good enough opponent to give him a run for his money and he'd ask her to play again some time. She turned and walked over to one of the other machines.

Time passed fairly quickly watching the kids play the machines and making comments about the games. Before she knew it, Penni's stomach told her it was time to eat. What time was it anyway? She stepped out into the Mall and looked at the clock shop across the aisle. At first she had found that shop to be of no help at all. There were clocks in the windows, on the walls, everywhere. Some were ticking and some were not. They all had different times. Finally, however, after weeks of looking she had picked out one clock that was a plain electric and always seemed to have the right time. She guessed that was the clock that the store used to set the other clocks by when it demonstrated or sold them.

Eleven-thirty! No wonder she was feeling hungry. She thought she'd go down to the "Bake and Fry" and see if she could find somebody to stake her to some food. The Bake and Fry was a quick food place on the corner of one of the turns. It had chairs and tables sitting part way out in the Mall floor. Some people stood at the counters on the inside and ate their food, others took it to the tables outside. It had already started to get crowded. She saw one of the guys she knew sitting at one of the tables with a fish fry plate. Good, she liked that.

"Hi!" Penni said slinging herself down into the extra chair at the table.

"Hi," he nodded.

Penni couldn't tell whether he was glad to have company or not. But that was the way with the Mall kids. They just expected you to be there so they didn't have to be glad when you were or sad when you weren't. They knew there would always be somebody there.

"I've got a fantastic secret!" Penni said. She leaned forward confidentially. "And I'll tell it to you if you promise not to tell anyone, and I mean *anyone*."

Her friend looked at her with a vaguely interested look. She motioned him to lean forward. "Well," she whispered, sounding as confidential as she could, "Now don't act surprised. I don't want anyone around to know I've even talked to you about this." She looked around. "But Mickey Mouse is coming here today!"

Penni leaned back nodding as if to confirm her information in case her friend could not believe it.

Her friend got a disgusted look on his face. Penni picked up one of his french fries, waved it in the air and then popped it into her mouth. "No kidding! It's the gospel truth. I saw the sign with my own eyes. Mickey Mouse, the one and only, the incredible, the fantastic, the impossible, the superextrafilstic, superexpecali—or whatever that thing is—Mickey Mouse will be right here in our very own Mall today."

Penni paused to let the full weight of her words sink in. While she was waiting for this to happen she picked up another french fry and popped it in her mouth. She leaned forward again. "I haven't told you the best part. He's been living in sin and he's bringing his sex partner with him ... yep Minnie!" She popped another french fry in her mouth. She paused again to let the weight of her words sink in. "And you want to know something else?" Penni leaned forward again.

"Oh, c'mon Penni, cut it out," her friend said.

"No," Penni said. "Now I am very serious about this. They say this place may even go to the dogs if Pluto comes...." She broke off a piece of his fried fish.

"Gimme that," her friend said grabbing at her hand. But she took evasive action and popped it in her mouth.

"Yep," she said. "If you think some of the people around here are quacks, wait till you see...."

"I know," her friend interrupted. "Donald Duck."

"Donald Duck." Penni nodded as if her friend had finally been enlightened and could now understand the marvelous truth she had been telling him. "I can't believe it," Penni waved her hands in pretend-excited animation. "The whole Disney crew is coming here today to see US!"

Her friend looked at her as if to say: what crazy thing are you saying now?

"Yes, to see US," said Penni. "We are as looney as a Looney Tune, as goofy as Goofy, as poopy as Snoopy, as jiggy as Miss Piggy...." Penni noted that he was starting on his second piece of fish. Before he could rescue it, she reached over and broke off another piece and popped it in her mouth.

"Penni, God damn it! Why don't you buy your own food?"

"Because," said Penni, "I like yours." She paused and then pretending to be alarmed quickly asked, "Why? What's wrong with your food?"

"There's nothing wrong with my food!" her friend retorted. "Except that I'm not getting very much of it with your ziggy hand coming in and out of it all the time."

"Then I won't have any more," Penni said. "I'll have a sip of your coke instead." And she picked up his cup and took a swallow.

Actually Penni had enough money in her pocket to buy an order of fries and coke. But no way was she going to spend that money on food. No, every cent she got had to be carefully saved and counted till she got enough for a bottle. Her friend at home was getting down and she needed more. Plus she wanted to have some with the gang tonight.

Penni was known as a "moocher." If she didn't kick in every once and a while, she knew they would eventually freeze her out. And she couldn't let that happen. She never did pay her fair share but she paid enough so they let her hang on. Even as it was, her Mom thought that Penni asked for too much money. "I never understand what you do with the money I give you," her mother often said. "Penni, you really should eat at home where there's good food rather than stuffing yourself with all those fries, cokes, and sundaes you keep telling me you buy at the Mall. You'd think now you'd be fat as a hen but I swear you're getting skinnier all the time."

Penni leaned back in her chair. The clock above the "Bake and Fry" order counter said 2:00. Penni stretched. Then she eased up out of her chair. "I think I'm going to cruise a bit."

Her friend nodded as he sipped his coke. "See you."

Penni made her way between the tables and chairs and started off toward Hearndon's. Hearndon's was the place where they had the best clothes. Well, the best clothes by Penni's standards. It was a store catering to young people. It played loud popular music and had flashing lights around the door. Penni never bought anything but she liked to look. Also it was very hard to tell her mother what she did at the Mall. She didn't like making things up and lying all the time. At least if she occasionally looked at Hearndon's she could tell her mother about some blouse or some skirt she had seen. Of course, it was obvious to Penni that looking at one blouse or one skirt did not take five or six hours. On the other hand, her mother seemed satisfied when she could say something about what she did.

Penni swung into Hearndon's. The sales girls there knew not to approach her and ask if she needed help. She had said "no" so many times and never bought anything so many times, they just let her alone. She sometimes wondered why they didn't just tell her to get out. Maybe they liked to see a familiar face. Or maybe they were just being polite. Or maybe they hoped she really would buy something someday.

Anyway, Penni wandered among the racks killing time. Occasionally she pulled something out and held it up against her in front of the mirror. Mostly she pulled out the kinds of things she knew her mother would never buy for her. She was doing that when she saw one of her girl friends outside the store motioning to her. Surprised she put the skirt back on the rack and hurried out.

"What's up?" Penni asked.

"Jack's got some stuff. C'mon."

"What's he got?"

"I don't know for sure. C'mon."

Penni hurried along with her friend. They left the Mall building and crossed over to the tree where Penni had waited earlier.

"Here," Jack dropped something in Penni's hand as she arrived.

"What is it?" Penni studied the small pills in her hand.

"Something real good," Jack said. "Go on. You'll love'm."

Penni took both pills. The others were standing with satisfied looks on their faces patiently waiting for the nice time ahead.

Pills are available from "street" dealers, the local drug store, or from the home medicine cabinet. They come in a wide variety of shapes, sizes, and colors. Pills obtained through illegal sources are notoriously unreliable as to dose and active ingredients. This can be dangerous to the user. Pills are classified by experts according to their action on the body. "Uppers" stimulate the body beyond normal limits—caffeine, cocaine (coke), and amphetamines (speed) are examples. "Downers" depress body functioning—opiates and barbiturates (barbs or reds) and have an action similar to alcohol. Hallucinogens (LSD, mes-

caline) *distort reality. Alcohol use in combination with any unprescribed pill and many prescribed pills may be dangerous. (Of the one hundred most frequently prescribed drugs, more than half are known to interact adversely with alcohol.)*

Someone cracked a joke. Penni thought it was very funny. Soon everything was funny. Penni felt her spirits soar. She twirled around and tapped her feet. What a good feeling. She began humming and singing to herself as she did her little dance. "M-I-C-K-E-Y M-O-U-S-E." She did a curvy side step. "Mickey Mouse, Mickey Mouse, he's the mouse for you and me. Oh, Mickey...."

Suddenly she stopped. "Hey everybody. Let's go see Mickey!"

"Mickey." Some of the others grinned.

"Yeah, I saw the sign," said Penni. "Mickey Mouse is going to be at the Mall today. C'mon."

"OK, let's go," someone said.

"Follow me," said Penni beginning the Mickey Mouse song again.

The kids grabbed onto each other forming a long line that snaked around between the cars. They all sang Mickey Mouse at the top of their voices as they followed along. When they arrived at the mall door, Penni turned. "Shhhhhhhh," she said, and pretended to look around like she wanted to surprise someone.

"Shhhhhhh," the rest said and imitated her behavior. Penni tiptoed into the Mall followed by the others.

Penni could hear voices coming from the stage. As she got to the center section she saw there was a big crowd. At least fifty mothers were sitting on the floor. Many had children in their laps as well as by their sides. Other mothers stood in back. Some held their children up so they could see. A person dressed as Mickey Mouse was on the stage along with a person dressed as Minnie Mouse. An announcer was asking them some type of dumb questions in response to which Mickey and Minnie were just shaking their heads.

"Hey, Mickey," Penni heard one of her friends suddenly

shout. "When you gonna marry Minnie? She looks eight months gone already to me!"

The announcer seemed a little startled but kept up with his patter. A good number of the mothers looked around and gave Penni and her friends chilling stares. The Mall kids grinned though.

Next the announcer announced Pluto was going to come up and do a dance. Someone appeared in a Pluto costume and began girating around to music.

"Look at Pluto—she's in heat!" another of Penni's friends yelled. "C'mon, Mr. Announcer, give it to her. Put her out of her misery. Can't you see, she's just gotta have it."

The announcer pretended not to hear but many of the mothers turned around and glared. The little kids turned around too, curious at who was yelling.

"Do it, man, we know you've got it in you—or are you afraid it's going to be too small when you take it out," yelled the Mall kids ignoring that Pluto was a male and much of what they were saying didn't make sense.

One of the mothers got up and taking her child by the hand, said "I'm going to find someone to get those kids out of here!" However, the child had no idea of why her mother was making her leave the show and she began to scream and cry.

Penni began to chant. "You scream, I scream, we all scream . . ." but instead of saying ice cream, she yelled "for you know what!" The others took up her cry.

"You scream, I scream, we all scream for you know what!"

"Will the people in the back, please be quiet!" pleaded the announcer.

"Shut up!" "Go away!" yelled some of the mothers. The children were standing up now looking toward the back.

"You scream, I scream . . ." the Mall kids continued. Then they took hold of each other and made the snake chain again. "You scream, kick, I scream, kick, we all scream for YOU KNOW WHAT!"

Suddenly men in suits came toward them. Penni felt herself being roughly shoved down one of the corridors along with the other kids. The men were shouting at them. Some of the children were running alongside trying to see what was going on. Mothers were calling. The whole place was in an uproar.

Penni felt the glare of the sun as they were shoved out of the nice cool Mall across the walkway and into the parking lot. She and her friends slowly assembled.

"Screw Disney World!" yelled one of the boys after the disappearing men.

"Snow White's cherry's got seven small dents in it!" yelled another.

That struck all the kids so terribly funny that they went laughing and staggering down the rows of cars. Penni laughed so hard the tears rolled down her face. She also felt some wet roll down her legs. She frowned. That was one trouble with drinking. You had to go a lot more and sometimes you went when you didn't expect to. Someone had a six pack of beer and they shared it. What they did and where they went after that became a blur in Penni's mind.

The next morning, by the look on her mother's face, Penni gathered that she must have come home late and that she must have been acting really high. Getting to where you felt really great and then just doing whatever you wanted to do, even if the next day you had no idea of what you had done, just sort of went along with the drinking in Penni's mind.

Sometimes Penni asked the other kids if she had had a good time. She loved to hear the tales about herself and what she had done. The gutsy kid in those stories was only a couple of pills or drinks away. Each day she tried to shorten the time in between.

Early signs of teenage alcoholism include being late for school and inability to pay attention while there, getting into trouble with school officials, driving while drinking, problems with friends, general personality change, losing control over the number of drinks consumed, and not remembering what was done during a drinking period (blackouts). Someone is physically dependent when he or she tries to stop drinking and experiences withdrawal symptoms which, in the beginning, usually involves involuntary shaking, headaches, insomnia, and general feelings of being very sick. At this point alcoholics need morning drinks to feel normal. Therefore one definition of alcoholism is a disease in which the ill person must consume large amounts of alcohol to feel normal—both from a physical and psychological standpoint.

7 ᭸ Jesse—Changes

For several weeks after he had gotten sick, Jesse avoided seeing the boys. It wasn't that they knew. It was just that he didn't like to think about it. And certainly he didn't want them pressuring him into having anything.

Also what seemed like a miracle had happened. Mr. Butterworth, one of Jesse's teachers at school had come by—made a special trip since Jesse didn't have a phone—and had told Jesse about a teenage employment program. Jesse had gone right down and had gotten a job. His job was to help fix up the playground and yard at an elementary school not far from his neighborhood.

Jesse was ecstatic. There just were no jobs to be had in the summer. Most of the kids didn't even bother to look. Not only did Jesse have a job for six weeks but it was something he liked too. Jesse had always been fond of little kids and the idea of helping fix up that old school appealed to him tremendously. They were going to pull all the weeds, straighten out the old fence—even put some new sections in it—plant some flowers and shrubs, and fix the playground equipment. There was only one swing that worked. And the joints were old and weak on the monkey bars. They were to help put in a new kind of climb-on-thing too. The man said it would be made out of big timbers and have tires that the kids could swing on.

Jesse and another boy were the main workers but there was a man who was to work with them and supervise them. Jesse was so happy. Over and over again he counted up how much money he would make and what he might do with it. The man had told him he probably wouldn't get paid till almost the end of the six weeks because this was a new government program. Apparently there was a lot of paper work before they would actually get the money to pay the kids. They could, however, order the equipment, tools, and stuff because they could get credit on that.

Every morning Jesse was up long before he had to be and arrived at the school extra early. He liked surveying the progress that had been made the day before and imagining how great it was going to be in the fall when the kids came back to school. He knew how happy he would have been if his own school had been spruced up to look like this one was going to look.

Jesse's mother kept asking him when he was going to get paid. Sometimes his mother did day work. But the people had gone away for the summer and didn't need her. Jesse and his mom had been trying to live off his dad's pension from the city. Jesse thought about the irony of it. His mom had left his dad—just taken Jesse and his brother and gotten out when Jesse was six. Jesse didn't blame his mom. His dad was a mean man, especially when he had been drinking. Lots of times his mom and dad used to drink together but then his dad had started drinking a lot more.

The effects of alcohol on judgement and self-control are such that anger and hostility which otherwise would not have been expressed, may come out forcefully. It is not known why some people become agitated when drinking and others become passive. Indeed the same person may act very differently after drinking depending on the mood and the setting. The largest American study on child abuse to date found that over a third of all child abusers had a history of problem drinking. Further drinking itself can be an issue which sparks disagreement and quarrels among family members.

Jesse's mom had gone to court to try to get his dad to give them money. Even though the court had said he should, he never would. One day he remembered his mother shouting, "Someday you're going to give me what you should whether you like it or not."

Jesse didn't see his dad much after that—only once or twice a year even though he didn't live very far from them. About four years ago, word had come that Jesse's dad had been killed. He worked for the sanitation department of the city and his truck had rolled back over him and killed him. Jesse didn't feel too much when his father died. He guessed his brother Tom felt more. Anyway it turned out his mom got a small widower's pension from the city. So it had all worked out. His dad was paying her all he had and he couldn't do anything about it. It really was strange the way it came about, just like his mom said.

For a while with the pension and his mother working they had managed. But then his mom had started drinking more. She had lost her regular job. Now she only had the part time work whenever she could get it. The pension wasn't really enough to keep them going and when his mom couldn't get work it was bad. Also it always seemed just at the time they didn't have enough money for his mom's drinking, she felt like she needed to drink more.

The largest economic cost of alcoholism in the United States is due to lost production of goods and services ($19.64 billion in 1975). Chronic drinking most often occurs among employed persons and their families. Most alcoholics are able to hold jobs because their families and employers look the other way and often actively try to hide the symptoms of alcoholism.

When Jesse's mom was into heavy drinking, Jesse tried to avoid her as much as possible. That was an extra reason to get to the school early even though he didn't have to. He often hung around after quitting time as well. When there was enough bread in the house, he would make himself two sandwiches, have one for lunch and then have the other for dinner, both in the school yard.

Sometimes as Jesse sat there in the school yard, he tried to imagine where Tom was. Had he really gone across the ocean? Was he in some foreign country now? He tried to picture what his brother would look like in a uniform. The country wasn't at war and Jesse didn't know what soldiers did when they weren't at war. He had seen army recruitment posters at the high school and in store windows. But the posters were confusing. They showed men sitting at computer consoles or dancing in clubs with nice looking girls. Was Tom out dancing somewhere or had he learned to push all kinds of buttons doing something? Did he ever think of them—especially of Jesse?

This day there had been no bread so Jesse just sat after work sketching in the dirt with a stick, drawing an imaginary picture of a push button machine. As he drew it got fancier and bigger and bigger. There were several computer panels with wire conduits leading off to other panels with levers and buttons. Before he knew it Jesse was really into his drawing. He jumped on his toes from one spot to another to avoid stepping on his drawing as the machine got bigger and bigger. More conduits, more panels, more consoles with data receivers and transmitters, more levers and buttons—finally he stepped back to look. His drawing was so big, he couldn't see it very well. He climbed up on the kids' monkey bars and balanced himself on the top. Then he slowly turned around and looked down.

It was magnificent! It covered almost a quarter of the playground and had wonderfully intricate panels and consoles and connecting wires. He stood admiring it. God what a machine! It was the biggest God damn machine he had ever seen. Finally he realized it just needed one thing. He jumped down and drew a small square box. He carefully drew two wires connecting the box to the machine. Then on the box he drew a button which he labeled *Go*.

Jesse paused. Now who should he draw standing there ready to push the button? Maybe Tom in his uniform! He started to draw. No, he scratched that out. It had to be somebody more important. A general with lots of stars! He started to draw again but then stopped. He had it. The president of the United States. That was it! He scratched his stick around in the dirt trying to make a man's image that looked like the president. But as he worked, he grew disgusted. No, that really wasn't who should push the button either. He stopped drawing, an annoyed look on his face. Suddenly he broke into a smile. Very deliberately he straightened his body. He paused a minute to square his shoulders. Then with his own finger he reached down and slowly pushed in the dirt button.

The electricity of Jesse's own brain waves seemed to momentarily crackle across the wires of the machine as the whole magnificent creation began to blink and work. It was fantastic. It was almost as if he could hear the whirring, whining noise as all the parts spun and flashed. The machine's noise grew in intensity until it was almost a screech. Gradually Jesse became aware the noise he was hearing was from a fire engine as it roared down the next street, not his machine at all. He stepped back. Oh well. That was one hell of a machine. Jesse smiled. It was starting to get dark. He backed out of the playground looking at his drawing. One hell of a machine. That was one hell of a machine.

Jesse stepped briskly along trying not to be aware of how hungry he was. Two more days and the pension check would come and then they could buy things again—at least for half the month. Jesse knew the cycle by heart.

As Jesse turned down the next street, he heard someone call out to him from an upper floor.

"Hey, your mom's pretty good at turning tricks. How about sending her up to me sometime."

Jesse stared up at the window but the voice came from inside and he couldn't see who said it.

"Show your face, you lying bastard," Jesse called.

"Don't get mad at me, sonny. I said I ain't had my chance yet," the voice called.

Jesse took a fix on the window and charged up to the apartment building door. But the downstairs main door was locked. He banged away at it but there was no answer and he couldn't get in. He charged back out to the middle of the street. "You take that all back, you lying bastard." But there was no response from the windows. Jesse yelled again. But all was quiet. He stood there helplessly for a minute. He fought back the tears. God damn it.

Jesse turned and went on down the street. He couldn't shake the bad feelings. By the time he got home he felt miserable. What he saw when he walked in the door made him feel even sicker. There were grocery bags on the table with groceries in them. And two days before the check was to come! Only a few of the groceries had been taken out of the bag and his mother was nowhere in sight. Jesse shut the door softly behind him.

"That you Jesse?" his mother's voice called from the living room. "I'm in here. C'mon in."

Jesse reluctantly passed through the kitchen and into the living room. His mother was sitting on the couch with a drink in her hand. The bottle was on the floor beside her.

"Mom, you promised you weren't going to drink again after the last time."

"Oh, it's just a little celebration. See the groceries?"

Jesse didn't say anything.

"Bet you're wondering how I got them, huh?"

Jesse looked at the floor.

"Well, I worked today at the Red Lion."

Jesse didn't say anything. He knew the Red Lion bar was a place not just for drinking but also for meeting.

"Well, aren't you going to ask me how I happened to work there?"

Jesse mumbled something.

"What's the matter with you, Jess," his mom said. "Well I was going by this morning and I saw a truck and they were unloading all these boxes. The owner was there and I stopped. I could see the boxes were full of glasses because they had pictures on the side.

"Getting new glasses?" I said. "Yes," said the owner. "Our old supply was getting pretty low and besides we're changing the size of the drinks today. Or supposed to be but these glasses are a week late." "Well," I said. "It's going to be hard to get those all unpacked and washed by opening time, if you want to start today." "Don't I know it," said the owner. "Well," said I, thinking fast. "I'd be glad to help. I wash up for the lady I work for but I'm not working today." Well the owner looked at me and asked if I could handle them without breaking them. "Would I be offering to do it, if I couldn't?" I said.

"Well, anyway, he just invited me right in. Said he'd pay me for every one I washed and dried and didn't break. And there were dozens and dozens and dozens of them. Of course he didn't have me put them all out. Some I just washed and put back in the boxes so he could get to them if he needed them. He also had me take down the old glasses and pack them away. By the time the bartender came to work I just about had it all done. Was he surprised to see his job done for him. And the owner paid me right on the spot. Said I had done a real good job. Said if he ever found he had to get another truckload of glasses in, he'd have me back to do them in a minute."

His mother had taken several sips of her drink while she was telling the story and now she took one long gulp and finished it off. She reached down for the bottle.

"Oh, mom, please don't," said Jesse.

Jesse's mother looked at him angrily. "Look, what I do is none of your business. You hear? If I want a drink I'll have a drink. You just be grateful I got some groceries. Now go fix yourself something to eat. There's plenty there."

Jesse stood silently. He wanted to say something to his mother but he couldn't think of how to do it.

"What's a matter with you, Jesse!" His mother's tone was really angry. "You just don't appreciate nothing. Here I work all day to get you something to put in your stomach and you go harping at me like I done something wrong. Go on, get out of here." His mother turned back to her glass and began filling it from the bottle.

Jesse watched a minute and then walked slowly back to the kitchen. He began to put the food away. He ended up putting it all away and leaving nothing out. As much as he was hungry, somehow the fact that he came across another liquor bottle mixed in the groceries, combined with his mother's drinking and what the voice had said, even if it wasn't true, left him unable to eat. He closed the cupboard door and went to sit on the back steps. He could hear the neighbor's television blasting away. Maybe that was what he would do with the money he earned. He might buy a television—theirs had broken. Once before when that had happened he had fixed it just by chance. He had taken the back off and wiggled all the tubes he could see. But the last time he had tried that it hadn't worked.

Jesse sat and listened all the way through "Star Journey" on the neighbor's TV. He couldn't always follow it. The voices were a small part of that show: a lot of it was special effects which if you couldn't see them didn't mean much.

"Jesse," his mother's voice interrupted him. The voice was cross and hollow. "Jesse!"

Jesse got up off the back porch and went in. He followed the sound of his mother's voice. She was still in the living room. "Jesse, where's that other bottle, I bought?"

Jesse gulped.

"Jesse," his mother's head wobbled and she slurred her words as she asked again, "Where's that other bottle I bought?"

"In the kitchen," Jesse answered.

"Get it for me."

"Ah, mom, don't you think you've had enough."

"Get it for me!" his mother's voice was harsh and angry even though she had trouble getting the words out.

"Ah, mom."

"Get it for me!" his mother yelled. As she did, she half

rose, picked up the empty bottle next to her and threw it at Jesse's head.

Jesse ducked. The bottle hit the wall and smashed. Glass showered over Jesse. A large piece flew back at Jesse and cut his cheek.

"Damn it," his mother said as she wobbled and sank back down on the couch. "Won't even get me the bottle." Then she keeled over on the couch and passed out.

Jesse stood trembling a minute. Then he shook himself gently. Pieces of glass that were stuck to his clothing fell tinkling to the floor. He looked at the glass on the floor and at his mom on the couch. Then he turned, went into her room, and got a cover. He took it over to her. His first instinct was to just throw it down on her. Instead, however, he tucked it in gently around her. He looked back at the glass on the floor. He just didn't have the heart to clean it up tonight. His mother would be sleeping it off till late in the morning so there was no danger of her getting up and walking on it. He'd get up and do it in the morning.

Passing out drunk is the result of the normal person drinking the equivalent of approximately one pint of whiskey and registering a blood alcohol level of 0.4 to 0.5 (0.1 is legally drunk). Alcohol is a depressant and an anesthetic and can literally put people to sleep. The liver will break down one drink per hour so the person who has had enough to pass out will still be under the influence well into the next day. For the nonalcoholic, death can occur at blood levels of 0.5 and higher. Alcoholics can remain functioning on larger doses because of their increased tolerance.

Jesse made his way back to his room. He didn't bother turning on the light. Instead he felt for his bed and fell down on it with his clothes on. He reached for the spot on his cheek where the glass had cut him and wiped away the blood with his hand. Outside he could hear rain beginning to fall. Suddenly he remembered the playground. His machine! What was going to happen to his machine! As the drops fell faster he could imagine them cutting into the wires of his drawing, rivulets of water running across the consoles. Suddenly he had a panicked feeling. The rain was going to destroy his machine! He sat up. He wanted to run back to the playground and rescue his machine. The noise of the rain falling outside his window beat in his brain. He knew it was hopeless. He turned his face into his pillow and buried it. His shoulders shook as he let out two huge sobs.

8 ～ Christine—Changes

Christine stayed in bed almost all morning. Every time she moved, her head pounded so that she thought it was going to break. She learned to move slowly and gently because rapid movement made it worse. She discovered bright light hurt her eyes so she pulled the window shades down. When she tried to amuse herself by turning on the radio, she found the sound hurt her ears so she turned it back off.

Eventually Christine managed to creep slowly to the bathroom. As she returned past the stairwell, she heard her mother's and dad's voices raised as if they were having a hot discussion.

"But Harry, don't you see," her mother was saying. "Christine has a *hangover!* She had drinks last night—alcoholic ones!"

"Well," she heard her father say briskly, "I think you're making too much out of this, Kathy. Christine didn't come home drunk last night. Whatever she had did not make her intoxicated. She can hold her liquor."

"But Harry, she's just a baby. She shouldn't be going out drinking."

"Kids are different today. They start everything much younger. Besides Christine didn't *go out* drinking. She was taken to a party where they served drinks. She had some. She has a headache. Didn't that ever happen to you?"

"But, Harry, Christine just should not be drinking."

"Look," Christine's father said. "Be glad she's drinking. She could be into marijuana or drugs. You wouldn't want that would you? A couple of drinks won't hurt her."

"Well, you're right, I suppose. I certainly would rather have her take a drink now and then than be on drugs. Well, maybe I shouldn't be hard on her."

"That's right," Christine heard her Dad's voice softening. "Christine's a fine girl. She's everything both of us ever wanted in a daughter. Let's not turn her against us by tightening the screws just when she may be feeling she needs some independence."

Parents probably still see alcohol use by their children as more acceptable than "drug" use because of the stigma attached to "drugs" and the fact that most parents drink themselves. Teenagers are aware that alcohol is less likely to get them into trouble with parents and the law. They see learning how to "hold their booze" as preparation for adulthood and many parents reinforce this belief. In 1977, over two-thirds of high school seniors expected to be drinking five years after graduation while only twenty-seven percent predicted they would be using marijuana five years in the future.

Parents would be wise to view alcohol and other drug use as a cluster of highly similar behaviors. Most young people today who get into trouble with one are likely to have problems with both. Experts working with these young people are beginning to use the term "chemically dependent" to replace the more traditional terms such as "alcoholic" and "drug addict."

Christine moved slowly back to her bed. She wasn't quite sure of all she had heard. It sounded a little as if they thought it was all right for her to drink. And why not, she suddenly thought. Everybody drinks. Whenever her mom and dad had company over, they always served drinks before dinner.

And there was wine with dinner, and after dinner drinks. And the country club served drinks. And there were drinks at weddings, christenings, funerals, drinks at her father's office parties. Everyone drank. There were Christmas drinks and New Year drinks, drinks on the Fourth of July and Labor Day. The whole world drinks and drinks all the time. So why shouldn't she drink?

Christine got slowly back into bed.

"Why not?" she mumbled to herself. "Why not?" Then she reached up to her head with her hand and answered herself. "Why not? I'll tell you why not—because of my head, oh, my head." The telephone beside her bed startled her. It sounded twice as loud as it ever had before. Christine reached to grab it as quickly as she could. She couldn't bear the thought of its ringing again. However, when she grabbed it, she moved too quickly and her head pounded terribly.

The "hangover" is not fully understood but some theories have been developed to explain it. Some authorities believe that acetaldehyde, one of the breakdown products of alcohol metabolism and a very toxic substance, is associated with the sick feelings following a drinking bout. The extreme sensitivity to lights, sounds, and movement are probably directly related to the depressant action of alcohol. The central nervous system adapts to receiving stimuli in a sluggish state and when alcohol is removed, a period of overexcitation is experienced. In the nonaddicted person the experience is uncomfortable but not dangerous. The alcohol dependent person experiences withdrawal symptoms often with extreme excitement of the nervous system. Withdrawal symptoms warrant prompt professional attention.

"Hello," said Christine weakly.

"Hi," said the voice on the other end. "I'm running a little late. So we'll be about ten minutes late in picking you up."

Christine frowned and tried to think. "Picking me up for what?"

"For what? The swim team race in competition with the Oak Hills Club!"

"Oh," said Christine, "I forgot all about it."

"Forgot all about it?" said the voice on the other end. "Christine how could you forget. Why you were the one dancing around at our extra practice shouting, 'We'll swim the gills off Oak Hills.'"

"Oh, I know," said Christine. "I just mean I forgot today. Oh, look," said Christine, "I can't go. You're going to have to go on without me."

"Go on without you? Christine we need you for the relay race. And you're the best girl swimmer in the medley."

"I know," said Christine, "and I'm sorry. But honestly I can't go. I'm sick."

"What's the matter with you?" the other voice asked.

Christine hestitated. "I've got the . . . the flu, I think. I've got terrible head pains and I can barely walk."

"Well, gee. I'm sorry, Christine. I'm really sorry. I'll tell the coach and the other kids. Hope you feel better. Bye."

Christine leaned over slowly and hung up the phone. She gradually turned back to her bed. All of a sudden she felt depressed. She had forgotten all about the swim team match and this was an important one. Christine wasn't the best swimmer in the world but it was her team's combined strength and steady performances that made them good. Other teams had some super stars but some really weak swimmers too. Christine's team were mostly all middle level good swimmers. Although they wouldn't get any of the individual medals this year, by accumulating points over the summer, they still hoped to come out as the top team.

Christine felt so helpless. She knew she really wasn't sick and should have been able to go. How stupid to be stuck with a hangover, she thought. Oh, why did I drink so much?

Along about mid-afternoon Christine began to feel better. She got out of bed, dressed, and went downstairs to watch the baseball game with her dad. He had opened up a can of beer. Christine rarely saw him drink more than one can. She looked at the golden beer as he poured some more in his glass. As strange as it seemed, it looked good to her. As a

Christine—Changes

matter of fact, she felt a slight craving for it. What is this, she thought. Here I am just getting over having too much and I feel like more. She shook her head questioningly. Regardless she wouldn't dare ask her dad for any.

The doorbell rang. "I'll get it," her mother said, coming downstairs. Christine heard the door open and male voices. Her mother called, "Christine, it's for you dear."

Christine turned around in time to see her mother escorting Arthur and Mark into the living room. "Hi," said Christine looking very surprised.

Her father turned his head, "Hi, boys, who you for? The Tigers or the Indians?" Then he added. "Although it may not matter, the way this game is going. It doesn't look like either team is going to do much."

Christine's father motioned the boys over. "Sit down and watch the game. C'mon."

"We can't stay," said Mark taking the seat next to Christine's father. "We just came by to say hi and Arthur wanted to ask Christine something."

"Oh, oh, look!" interrupted Christine's dad. "Just as I said they weren't going to do anything, look at that! A homer with a man on!"

Arthur sat on a chair next to Christine. "Look," he started, "I'm sorry to butt in without calling first, but we were just driving around, and I got a really great idea. Tomorrow Mark's going to go off golfing and while he's doing that, I thought that you might like to go riding with me. He says there's a nice trail around Sutter's Hill."

"Well," said Christine. "I have swim practice in the morning."

"What time do you finish?"

"Around 11:00."

"Well then, we would make it a picnic lunch somewhere on the trail."

Christine chewed on her lip. She had been taking riding lessons so she could sit a horse but she didn't know about the kind of high-spirited horses Arthur rode.

She hesitated. "I don't know," she said. "I'm not really used to riding the kind of horses you ride."

"Oh," said Arthur. "I wouldn't take any of the Morgans out on the trail—it would ruin them. No, we'll use trail horses. There are some over at the show barns."

"Well," said Christine. The idea of going out with Arthur was certainly appealing. Surely she'd feel much better by tomorrow. "OK I guess, it's OK. Let me check first with mom to make sure she hasn't got anything planned." Christine figured it wouldn't hurt if she skipped her Monday afternoon art lesson. "I'll be right back."

Christine tracked her mother down in the kitchen and got her approval. "Sure, that's fine," said Christine returning to the living room. "I'll be home and ready by 11:30. Is that all right?"

"Great," said Arthur. "C'mon Mark, I'm ready to go."

Mark got up from his seat reluctantly. "Did you see that?" he said to Arthur still looking at the TV. "The coach held that man up at third and it was a short throw. I'm sure he could have gotten home."

"Well, can't do anything about it now," said Arthur.

"Yeah, OK," said Mark and he smiled at Christine. "You gonna go?"

"Yes," said Christine.

"That's great," said Mark. "Thanks."

Christine wanted to say, "Thank me? Goodness, Thank you. Going out with Arthur is fantastic." But she just smiled casually and said, "You're welcome."

Christine saw them to the door and out. After she had closed the door, she stood with her back to it holding on to the door knob. A huge smile spread across her face. Here she was going out with an older guy again. He had actually asked her out again. How fantastic.

It was a pretty summer day—not too hot—as Christine and Arthur guided their horses along the trail. Christine was grateful for that. She didn't want to get hot and sweaty riding along. She wasn't wearing any perfume to cover the smell.

She'd made that mistake one time. Christine had worn her best flowery perfume on a picnic. She had spent half the picnic batting at bees and running away from them. She had even stood in the smoke of the cookout fire hoping that would keep her safe. However, she had only ended up getting her lungs full of smoke. The second half of the picnic she'd spent in the car with the windows rolled up. Oh, was it hot in there. But even when she rolled down a window just a crack, a bee would crawl in.

"That must be the spot Mark meant was good for a picnic," Arthur said pointing to a grassy area near a two-foot waterfall. "He said if we followed the creek trail for about half an hour we'd come to a little waterfall with some nice grass near it."

They turned their horses off the trail.

"Let's tie up here," said Arthur and cross over by ourselves to the other side. We don't want to be too near these guys when we eat."

They tied their horses. Arthur took the big picnic basket he had tied on behind his saddle and reached for Christine's hand. "C'mon. It looks like we can cross up here."

Arthur guided Christine along the grassy bank and then helped her carefully step from stone to stone across the small creek. The water was down from lack of summer rain and Christine could see that even if they had fallen in, it wasn't more than eight or ten inches deep. However, she didn't want to get her riding boots wet so she balanced herself as carefully as she could.

"Here's a good spot," said Arthur, leading her back under a low spreading tree. Arthur spread out the picnic blanket. From where they were, they couldn't see the horses or the trail. It was quiet and peaceful. The sun winking through the trees spread pretty patterns over the blanket. Christine sat down.

"Mark's mom and dad had a party Saturday night and these are the leftovers," Arthur said opening the picnic basket. He took out some tiny sandwiches, cheese, little vegetables and a party dip, small bite-size party cakes, two glasses and a large bottle of wine. There was water dripping down the side of the bottle so Christine could see that it had been chilled.

"Wine!" Christine said in surprise.

"Why yes," said Arthur naturally. "You didn't think I was going to bring beer for an elegant picnic with you, did you?" He leaned over and gave her a quick kiss on the cheek and then took out the corkscrew and began opening the bottle.

"Why no," said Christine. She could have added, I would have thought we'd just have coke or something, but she didn't.

"I got a fairly sweet wine," he said. "I didn't know whether you liked your wine dry or not, but I hate dry wines with frosted stuff." He motioned toward the sweet party cakes.

Wines differ widely in their taste based on the fruit used and the type of fermentation and aging. Effects of wine on the body are not significantly different from the effects of other alcoholic beverages. Alcohol content varies but most wines average about twelve percent. However champagne and other sparkling wines enable alcohol to be absorbed more quickly than regular wine. A "wino" is an alcoholic who prefers wine usually because of its low cost relative to distilled spirits.

"Here, try this," he said, handing Christine a glass of wine.

Christine hesitated. It was pink and the sun on it in the glass made it sparkle. It really was pretty to look at. Christine had never been at such an elegant picnic before. It seemed like something out of a romantic novel. She put the glass to her lips and took a dainty sip. It had an interesting flavor. The coolness felt very good on her throat. Surely this would not affect her the way the hard liquor had. It was light—almost like pop.

Arthur raised his glass. "To a lovely flower that I didn't expect to find blooming in this part of the country." He smiled and sipped his wine too.

Christine felt herself blush a little. She tossed her head, smiled, and took another sip. Arthur stretched his legs out and leaned back on one elbow. "Now this is the life: a good horse, a beautiful day, a pretty girl . . . and Mark's mother's party leftovers," he added, laughing. Arthur reached over, got a carrot curl, dunked it in the dip and put it in his mouth. "Have some," he said.

Christine was hungry after swimming. She picked up one of the tiny hors d'oeuvre sandwiches. It seemed to be a mixture of smoked ham and something else. There was a tiny anchovy on top. She picked that off. "Do you like these?" she said.

Arthur shook his head, "No."

"Me neither."

Arthur reached in the picnic basket and pulled out the bag the sandwiches and vegetables had been in. "Here, we can use this for trash."

Christine dropped the anchovy in the bag, then pushed back against the trunk of the tree. She spread a napkin in her lap and rested the tiny sandwich on it. She was afraid to put her wine glass down for fear it might tip over on the ground so she held it and took some more sips. Out beyond the tree branches she could see a bit of sky and then more trees as they crowded in to get a drink at the side of the creek. "I wonder how this little spot got to be so grassy when the trees are so close to the bank of the creek the rest of the way."

"Hmmm," mused Arthur munching on a stuffed olive. "I don't know." He took another swallow of his wine, emptying his glass. "Here have some more," he said, picking the bottle up out of the basket and filling her glass as well as his own. "Do you like it?"

"Yes," she said. "Very nice." As they sat and talked and drank, Christine began to get a mellow good feeling. The world seemed less sharp but much lovelier. She grew fascinated with the ripples the wind made in the creek water. "Oh, this is special," she sighed.

"You're special," said Arthur taking her almost empty glass from her hand and setting it in the picnic basket. He leaned over, embraced her and kissed her deeply. Christine pressed his lips back warmly. They kissed a long time. Then Arthur moved back to his position. He reached in the picnic basket, took out her glass, and filled it again.

Christine took the glass and began sipping more wine. Surely this must be a dream, Christine thought, sipping wine with this handsome stranger from another state on this gorgeous day.

This time when Christine emptied her glass, she held it out for more. She had such a great floaty feeling, she wanted to make sure it wouldn't go away. Arthur emptied the bottle into her glass. Christine watched the last two drops fall gently into the rolling liquid. She couldn't believe they had drunk the whole bottle of wine themselves. It seemed like so much when he had taken it out. Now she wished he had brought another one.

Arthur put the bottle down. "Have some dessert," he said and passed her a tiny frosted cake.

She took several more sips of wine and then bit into a cake. She wasn't sure she liked the taste of the cake and the wine together. The cake was too sweet. "I don't think I want any more of that," she said. "I'll just finish my wine."

When she had finished it, she handed her glass to Arthur and stretched out on the far side of the blanket. "Mmmmm," she said, "that was a delicious picnic."

The mellow or floaty feeling experienced after using alcohol is the direct result of depression of the central nervous system. Young people should know that there are many other ways of achieving this "high" feeling so that they have alternatives to drugs and alcohol if they want to experience an altered consciousness or relax. For example, meditation and other deep relaxation experiences can promote a feeling of relaxed well-being and peace. Becoming involved in painting or other artwork, music, or writing can help achieve a feeling of concentration related to the dreamy aspects of life rather than the more rational day-to-day problems.

Arthur shoved the leftovers in a bag and put them in the picnic basket along with the glasses and empty bottle. "You've got a little bit of frosting at the corner of your mouth," he said.

She raised her hand to brush it off. "No," he said reaching over and catching her hand. "Let me do it." He moved to her side and lay down next to her and began kissing her.

Christine wanted very much to be kissed. The floaty feeling she had left her relaxed and willing. She kissed as meaningfully as he kissed. Then she felt his hand sliding over her chest and breast. She pushed upward. She wanted to be felt harder. Before she knew it, he had slipped his hand under her stretch top and inside her bra and was feeling her skin directly.

It felt so new and strange. Christine had never let anyone do that before. With the motion of his hand and his kissing, however, she felt like she wanted more. And she felt so mellow. It was as if her will to resist was just not what it usually was and somehow that didn't matter.

Alcohol is associated with romance in our society. It is often marketed that way by manufacturers in their advertising. Drinking can lead to an atmosphere where emotions are felt more intensely and expressed more readily. In general, however, the effect of alcohol on one's sexual desire is an individual matter. In treatment centers for alcoholics, one does hear girls and boys discuss regret over one night stands they became involved in during heavy drinking. Some describe waking up with a member of the opposite or same sex and not recalling how it all came about. In general, since alcohol is a depressant drug, it decreases overall sexual performance and dulls some of the pleasurable feelings associated with sexual contact. Heavy drinking can result in impotence.

Christine could hear Arthur starting to breathe faster. His body was moving too. She felt his hand reach down and go inside her riding pants. Christine held her breath, wanting more, yet not wanting more.

As Arthur's hand reached down lower, however, something in her seemed to wake up. She broke off the kiss.

"No," she said and reached for his hand. Arthur stopped his hand where it was but didn't take it out. He tried to begin kissing her again.

Christine broke off the kiss. "No," she said and this time pulled out his hand.

Arthur rolled over on his back. Christine sat up.

"I'm sorry, Arthur." She tried to think of what else she should say. Should she say "I'm not that kind of girl"? "I just don't want to do that"? "I'm not protected"? "I've never done it before"? She felt inadequate, a disappointment to him. He didn't look at her. He just lay there staring out under the branches. She thought momentarily of letting him go ahead. But the mood had been broken and she really didn't want to. Yet she felt as if she owed him some explanation.

Finally she said, "Look, I like you but I really don't know you that well, and . . . well tomorrow you'll be going back to your own state and we might never ever see one another again."

He turned and looked at her. "That's why I want to," he said softly. "I want something to remember you by because I might not see you again and I find you very exciting.

"But that's why I don't want to," Christine said, "because I may never see you again."

"OK," he said, rolling over on his back again, not looking at her.

Two tasks to be accomplished in moving from childhood to adulthood: developing a personal identity and independence from adult control and selection of a means of supporting oneself have already been discussed. Three other tasks are dealing with bodily changes, establishing a sexual identity, and developing a system of values. During adolescence the bodies of boys and girls mature rapidly. Sexual characteristics either develop or become more pronounced. Young people have to deal with changed body images along with increased physiological pressures toward sexual behavior. Deciding "what it means to be a man" and "what it means to be a woman" becomes an important interplay in most activities. Young people also develop a system of values. Part of this process is critically examining the values of adults close to them, those expressed in the broader society, and those of peers.

How far to go in sexual relationships, whether or not to drink and how much to drink, all have to do with the set of values the young person is developing or has developed. Many adolescents need to experiment and experience before they can decide what is right for them.

Christine sat next to Arthur feeling very awkward. She wasn't sure what to do next.

Finally Arthur said, "Well, let's go."

Christine got up off the picnic blanket and stood feeling very ill at ease. Arthur picked up the picnic basket and the blanket and walked ahead of her across the stream. How different it was than on the way over when he had carefully held her hand so she wouldn't fall in.

Christine followed. The wine affected her balance. Twice her foot slipped off a rock and she was forced into the water. Getting her riding boots wet further added to the uncomfortableness Christine was feeling.

When they got back to the horses, Arthur silently fixed the picnic basket and blanket on the back of his saddle and then got up. Christine mounted her horse too. Arthur started his horse moving back to the trail without saying anything. When he got to the trail, however, he paused momentarily as if undecided about which way to turn. Christine didn't know what to think. If he turned to the right, they would be going back the exact way they came and their ride would be over very shortly. Surely that would end their relationship on a very quick and sour note. On the other hand, she didn't look forward to jogging silently after him for another hour or so. There was something degrading about following along behind someone who was ignoring you.

Suddenly Arthur turned his horse to the left and started off at a trot. Christine had no choice but to follow. The trail wound around and eventually they got to a place where they could gallop. Christine galloped after him. The motion didn't set well with the wine. Any remaining floating feelings got bounced out.

Finally they came to a place in the trail with an overlook. Arthur pulled his horse over to look out. She stepped her horse slowly in next to him and looked out too.

"This is a nice view," Arthur said suddenly. "Mark didn't tell me about this."

"Yes it is pretty," Christine answered.

Suddenly Arthur looked at her. "About back there," he said. "It's OK. I don't like my girls to be too fast. Can we just forget it?"

Christine looked at him. "OK," she nodded. "It's forgotten."

"Well then," said Arthur, "Let's have a nice ride the rest of the way around the hill. Mark said he'd meet us back at the horseshow barns at 4:30."

Christine had forgotten that Arthur didn't have a car of his own and Mark had dropped them off before he had gone golfing. It also suddenly dawned on her that a golf game didn't take to 4:30.

"What's he going to do after the golf game—a game doesn't take that long."

"Oh, he'll probably sit around and have some beers at the course. I don't know what he'll do but he said not to worry, it would be OK to pick us up at 4:30."

The thought vaguely crossed Christine's mind that Mark might have known what Arthur was going to try to do or that they even might have cooked it up together. But Arthur was already turning his horse.

"C'mon," he said, "the trail ahead looks interesting."

Christine followed. Now that Arthur had spoken to her she felt much better. She would have hated to have had to finish out the day on such a bad note. It wasn't a perfect day any more but at least it wasn't as bad as it had been a while ago.

When Christine and Arthur reached the barns, they had their horses stabled. Even though they were several minutes late, Mark still wasn't there when they finished.

"Where could he be?" said Christine. "Do you think he forgot?"

"No," said Arthur. "He's probably just been having a good time." As he said that, they heard the squeal of tires and a car sped into the entrance of the parking lot.

"There he is now," Arthur said. The car came bumping across the lot raising dust and flinging rocks.

"Why's he coming so fast?" Christine asked. "He's not that late."

The driver of the car suddenly applied the brakes and the car swerved to a stop. Stones and pebbles flew out from under the tires. They showered against Christine's riding boots.

"C'mon," said Arthur, opening the rear door and throwing the picnic basket blanket in ahead of him, "Let's get in."

"Oh, hi Sandra!" Christine said in surprise when she saw who was in the front with Mark.

"Hi," said Sandra.

"Everything work out OK?" said Mark to Arthur with a grin on his face.

"Yeah, super," said Arthur. "That's a really nice trail."

"Well, I always say a little riding is good for everybody," Mark said turning back to the steering wheel and gunning the car motor. "Where to everybody?"

"I have to get home," said Sandra.

"So do I," said Christine.

"Well, then, home, home, home!" said Mark with a carefree toss of his head. He let up on the clutch so that the car spun crazily sideways as he started out.

Christine gripped the side handle on the rear door as the car careened out of the parking lot. She had never seen Mark in such a mood. And Sandra seemed to be practically the same way.

"Vroom, vroom, vrooom," said Mark as he shifted into third and then fourth, accelerating all the while.

Christine watched the telephone poles whizz by as they sped down the highway. "Mark, don't you think you're going too fast?" Christine asked. "This is a forty mile an hour zone and you're going over fifty-five." Mark also was straying over the center line.

Sandra turned around. "Don't worry, Christine, Mark's a great driver."

Christine looked at Sandra. Her face was flushed. She was obviously high and didn't recognize the danger in their wild ride. The car swerved and it seemed to Christine, Mark had real trouble getting it back under control.

"Arthur?" Christine looked at him, hoping he might say something to Mark. But Arthur just smiled at her, shrugged, and looked out his window. He either was getting a kick out of it or didn't want to interfere with Mark.

Alcohol can give one a false sense of control. Also alcohol slows reaction time to critical situations such as those that often occur while driving. The risk of an accident increases with each drink the driver has consumed. The use of marijuana and other drugs increases the chances of a crash. Since teenagers are often under many constraints at home and at school, they value driving as a symbol of independence and the highway as a place to "let loose." Pairing this tendency with alcohol abuse results in serious problems. It is estimated that nearly 8,000 young people die in alcohol-related auto accidents each year. Some 40,000 more are injured in these accidents.

Christine felt helpless, trapped. Mark was not handling the car well. She could feel he was fighting to control it on the turns. He couldn't seem to tell when he was speeding in control and when he was speeding nearly out of control. Christine gripped the sides of her seat cushion. I hope we get home soon. She tried to measure in her mind whether or not they were at least half way home. How much further did they have to go?

They shot out past a car and cut quickly back in front of it. The driver of the other car blew his horn at them angrily. "Whooo, whoooooo!" said Mark and Sandra laughed.

Christine could tell Mark and Sandra had been drinking. Mark had had drinks at the Danvers' party the other night too, but he hadn't acted this way.

By now, Christine was really scared. What if he crashes? Christine peered anxiously over the seat, out the front window, trying through her concentration to help Mark drive. I'll never get in the car with him again, thought Christine, if only I can get home now.

Finally the car stopped at Sandra's house. "Sandra, I'm coming in with you," Christine said, getting out of the car the same time as Sandra.

"OK," said Sandra somewhat puzzled. She looked confused. "But Mark will take you home."

"I just need to call my parents and I wanted to...." Christine couldn't think of anything else to say.

Mark gunned the motor. "Well, are you coming or aren't you coming?"

Christine leaned over and looked in the backseat car window. "Thanks for taking me on the picnic, Arthur. I hope you have a good trip home." Then she turned to Mark. "You go on, Mark. I need to do something here and I'll get another ride home."

"OK," said Mark with a shrug of his shoulders. "So long."

"Bye Christy," said Arthur, as the car began to move down the drive.

"How come you wanted to come in?" asked Sandra.

Christine still could not believe Sandra didn't know. "Oh, I had to go to the john real bad and I was afraid I couldn't wait."

"Oh sure," said Sandra, "I know what you mean. C'mon in."

"Mom, I'm home," shouted Sandra as they entered the house. "Christine's with me. We're going upstairs to the john." The girls went upstairs. "You can use that one," Sandra said. "I'll use the one in my parents' bedroom."

Christine walked into the bathroom.

"Ooopse," said Sandra, ducking in behind her. "I need to take this with me," and she grabbed her toothbrush and toothpaste.

That reminded Christine that she probably smelled like she had been drinking too. She didn't want to go home that way. She wished she had a breath mint or something with her. Since she didn't, however, she peeked inside the medicine cabinet over the sink. There was a bottle of mouthwash sitting on the shelf. She took it out, poured some into the bathroom glass, and gargled several times.

That ought to do it, she thought, carefully rinsing out the bathroom glass and putting it back in the holder. She dried off her hands and went into Sandra's room to use the phone. Sandra was not back from the other bathroom yet.

The phone at Christine's house rang a long time. Oh, please be home, Christine thought to herself. Finally her mother answered. She sounded a bit breathless.

"Mom, I'm at Sandra's. Can you come and pick me up?"

"Christine, I just this minute walked in the door. I really don't feel like going back out. I thought you said Mark and his friend would be bringing you back home."

"I did, mom, but they dropped us off at Sandra's instead."

"Well, that wasn't very nice. I think, Christine, when you accept a date it should be with the understanding that your date will see you home. What kind of boys are these?"

"Well, mother, they would have. . . . Mom, could you just come and pick me up please?"

"Christine, when I was young, any boy. . . ."

"Mom, please, will you come and pick me up?" Christine's voice sounded exasperated and urgent.

"Well, all right, Christine. But I've got to put the meat and the milk in the refrigerator first."

"OK mom, I'll wait. Goodbye," Christine said and hung up the phone.

Parents have a responsibility to communicate with their children about the subject of drinking and driving. Parents and young people should come up with a set of rules to follow and possible ways to handle drinking and driving situations that might occur. A parent should let his children know that calling home for a ride or calling a cab is a better option than accepting a ride with someone who has been drink-

ing. Other options include offering to drive for someone who has been drinking or staying overnight at a party-giver's home. After parent and teenager have had this discussion all will feel much better and will in fact be much safer.

Of course, the best practice is to not mix drinking with driving at all.

Christine sat down on the edge of Sandra's bed. She was still shaken from the ride. She never wanted to do that again.

Sandra walked back into the room and flung herself happily down on the bed. "Mark is so neat," she said. "We had the most fantastic time this afternoon. I mean really fantastic. I just can't believe it."

Christine looked at her. Something was different about Sandra, Christine felt.

"And you know what? He asked me if I'd like to go to the summer cotillion with him next Saturday."

Christine tried to appear happy for Sandra. She hated the way Mark had driven the car. At the same time getting invited to the cotillion was very special. Sandra was certainly moving up fast in the older circle. Christine didn't know what to say. Sandra's life now seemed so removed from hers. Christine was glad when her mother came and she didn't have to talk to Sandra any more.

9 ∽ Penni—Changes

As the weeks passed, Penni felt herself getting caught in an ever greater pinch. Her bottle at home seemed to be forever running out. She never could remember drinking that much out of it—but it always seemed to need replacing. Now she couldn't go a day without having a drink. She needed one in the morning. Most often, late afternoon became an agony. She lived until she could have one in the evening.

The need for more alcohol comes from the development of tolerance. Developing tolerance is a major sign of alcoholism. Tolerance develops over time and is defined as needing increasing amount of the drug to obtain the desired effect. The alcoholic finds that he or she is drinking more and enjoying it less. Tolerance is not just something that happens with alcohol but is associated with most drugs. The body makes adjustments so it can function as close to normal as possible despite alcohol ingestion. These adjustments work against the depressant effect of alcohol and more must be consumed to obtain the effect. For the alcoholic drinker, this means daily drinking and keeping alcohol in the blood around the clock. Of course when a person who is a heavy drinker is sleeping he cannot drink and therefore his blood alcohol levels begin to drop and by morning he may be having some with-

drawal symptoms. The body seeks to compensate by signaling a need to drink again. When alcohol is removed, the body is in an overexcited state. There is a tremendous need to drink to feel normal again. Craving may be related to dropping levels of alcohol in the blood but it also can be primarily a psychological symptom. It can reflect a need to escape an uncomfortable feeling or it may be a conditioned response triggered by someone or something that is associated with drinking.

Penni's mother expected her to watch her brother now that he was out of church camp so she couldn't always go to the Mall. Freddie was a good kid. However, she was afraid he might find out she was pill-popping and drinking and tell someone. Also her mother was getting suspicious about the money she needed. Somehow Penni had to come up with her own supply of cash.

Alcohol habits are expensive. However, the cost varies in terms of the wide variety of beverages available and the differences in tolerance among individuals. An average cost might run between five and ten dollars a day at current prices. Since young people most often don't have a source of money independent of their parents, paying for alcohol can become a problem. They may find themselves in a pattern of asking for money to go to the movies or other activities and using the cash for drinking. Since the amount of alcohol must be increased over time to get the desired feeling, relying on parents for money often is not enough. Many times young people will sell their possessions, such as bikes, tape recorders, even clothes.

Finally, one morning Penni heard her mother talking on the phone about needing to get her new father a birthday present. "But I can't take any extra time off work," her mother said. "This is our busy time. I thought I could get the one I wanted in the store near the office but they're sold out. I don't know how I am going to get it by Saturday without his knowing. I don't want to put it on my charge either because I don't want him to know how much I paid for it. Otherwise I could just call someplace and have them send it out."

"Listen," said Penni to her mother as soon as she hung up the phone, "I can go over to the Mall and get it for you. I'm sure they have it over there."

"Well, it's a fairly expensive kind of robe I want to buy him." Her mother hesitated. "Do you think you can manage all that cash?"

"Sure," said Penni. "I know all the stores and I am sure one of them will have it."

"Well, if you could do that for me, Penni, it surely would be a help," her mother said. "I've got the money for the robe in my purse right here. And here's another twenty-five dollars. Why don't you buy something for you to give him and something for Freddie to give him."

"OK, mom," said Penni. She couldn't believe her mother was putting this enormous amount of money in her hand rather than the little bit here and there, she usually got.

"This might be a good day to go," said her mother. "Your aunt's bringing your cousin over to play with Freddie today and she'll be here through lunch. And I do want you to know that I appreciate your looking after Freddie most days. I know you need a break once in a while. And I know you like to go to the Mall so why don't you do it today."

"Great, mom," said Penni.

Penni waited impatiently until her aunt came. "Don't you want to wait until after lunch, Penni?" her aunt had asked as Penni was going out the door.

"No," said Penni, "I'm not hungry and I have some special shopping to do for my mom."

"Yes, I know," her aunt had said. "But I thought you might wait and have lunch with us. I don't get to see you that often."

"Oh, I'll be back before you go," Penni had said and had shut the door before her aunt could say anything else.

All the way over to the Mall, Penni calculated how she would go about it. She needed the money for herself, that was for sure. That would mean she wouldn't have to sweat money for a month or maybe even more. The trick was exactly how she was going to do it so she could have the money and her mother would never know. It had to take careful planning and some guts. She wished she had had time for a little extra from her bottle before she left. However, she hadn't and what she had had this morning would have to do.

Penni entered Feldstone Department Store. First she had to locate the merchandise. She went to Feldstone's because they were the most logical store to have an expensive robe.

"May I help you?" said a clerk.

"No thank you," said Penni. She didn't want anyone to point out the merchandise to her unless absolutely necessary. "I'm just looking."

Penni looked over the counter displaying robes in neat plastic bags. No. No luck. The robe wasn't there.

The clerk was standing by watching her. "We also have some robes hung up on hangers over there, if you'd like to look at those." She started over toward the rack.

"That's fine," said Penni waving her hand. "I can go over and look myself." Sure enough, there was the exact robe her mother had told her to get. It was on a hanger. OK so they have it, thought Penni. She wasn't sure whether or not the clerk was still watching her. She didn't want to appear too interested in any one thing so she gradually browsed her way out of the department.

The next thing was to get a bag. It had to be a Feldstone's bag and it had to be big enough that she could get the robe in quickly. If anything went wrong having the robe in a Feldstone's bag gave her a better chance of getting out of it by saying it was a gift she was returning. Also if she looked like a Feldstone customer who already had a purchase, she would be less suspicious.

Penni knew the linen department would have fairly big bags because they sold pillows, comforters, and other large items. Also she knew that often they were quite busy. Penni took the escalator up to the second floor. There were several customers in the linen department. A clerk was ringing up a sale at the cash register. The bags were kept under the counter with the cash register on it. Penni pretended to look at the pillow cases on a counter close by. "Here's your change," Penni heard the clerk say, "and thank you." She put the sheets and pillow cases the customer had bought in a big bag and handed them to the woman.

Another woman moved up to the cash register. "Could you help me, please. I wanted to look at these bedspreads over here." The clerk moved away from the cash register.

Penni's heart began to pound. She glanced around. The clerk was still walking away. The only other clerk was in the corner with her back turned. Penni darted behind the counter and pulled out a bag. As she did so she saw some discarded plastic pillow wrappers under the counter. She grabbed a handful. Then she ducked away from the cash register and behind a display of curtains. Quickly she opened the bag and plumped it out. The noise was the loudest thing she had ever heard. However, she felt she had to sacrifice noise for speed. She shoved the plastic in and folded down the top of the bag.

Suddenly two feet appeared under the curtain display next to hers. Penni stood momentarily frozen. They couldn't accuse her of stealing anything. She wasn't even near a counter. Penni reached out and fingered a curtain as if she were looking at the quality. Then she took her bag and moved off toward the down escalator. She never knew whether the person on the other side of the curtains was a clerk or a customer. The shoes stayed and did not follow her.

Once downstairs Penni moved to the cosmetic section which was located across the aisle from the men's clothes. Men's clothes still wasn't busy. The clerk stood with her hips resting against a counter staring vacantly. It was obviously a slow day for her.

Penni knew there was no way she could do anything with the clerk just standing there like that. Good. A customer was going into the men's department. Penni saw the clerk move forward. Now was her chance. But something told her to wait. The clerk and the customer talked earnestly for a minute and then the clerk shook her head. The customer said something and then walked out of the department.

Good lord, Penni thought. This could go on all day. She was getting a bit anxious. She studied some lipsticks in the case intently. Fortunately the cosmetic department was busy so no one had yet come to help her. Suddenly out of the corner of her eye, she saw the men's clerk begin walking over to the counter where she was looking. She grabbed her bag tighter. She wanted to turn and walk away but she thought that would be too obvious. She studied the lipsticks more fiercely than before.

The clerk walked by her and around the counter to where a cosmetic clerk was waiting on a woman. "Hey," she heard the men's clerk say. "Listen, I don't know what was in that omelet I had for breakfast but my stomach is very upset. I've just got to get something for it. I'll be right back. Here's the key to the cash drawer but, honest, I don't think you'll have to do anything. It hasn't been busy today at all. And it will only take me a couple of minutes."

Penni could see the other clerk nod and take the key. Then the cosmetic clerk went back to writing up the sale for her customer. Penni could not believe her luck. She watched the clerk make her way across the floor toward the escalator.

As casually as she could, Penni moved across into the men's department. She went directly to the robe section. She took one quick look around. Then she opened her bag and held it under the robe. Her heart was pounding. She reached up and tugged at the robe. It wouldn't come off the hanger. She tugged again. The robe came partly off the hanger but then stuck. She gave another urgent tug. One end of the hanger swung up but it still didn't come. Penni pushed aside the robe next to it. She thought of giving up. She took another quick look around. Still no one this side of the cosmetic counter and no men's department clerk. She gave a final desperate tug. The robe slipped off. She caught it and shoved it into the bag. She quickly rolled the bag down again. Then she strode purposefully across the department and out into the aisle.

It seemed to take forever to get out of the store and into the mall. All the time, Penni imagined people were coming after her. She hurried toward the center of the Mall and took the escalator up. She felt like she needed to sit down. She went to the Bake and Fry and popped in an empty chair. She knew they didn't like you sitting there if you weren't eating. But she just needed to sit down a minute. Whew! Did she need a drink! No, she thought, no drink. I've got to get the rest over first. However, sit a minute, she told herself. Sit just one more minute.

OK, Penni finally said to herself. Two more gifts to go. But maybe they wouldn't be so hard.

Penni took the escalator back down to the first floor. At least she was at the opposite end of the Mall from Feldstone's.

Candy was at her check-out station at Rickles. Penni glanced at the sign by the "in" turnstiles. It said, "All parcels must be opened for inspection before leaving the store or left with the clerk upon entering." Penni hesitated, then holding her Feldstone's package above the turnstiles, she pushed on into the store with it. Candy was busy with checking out and did not see her enter. Penni thought it would seem more odd if she interrupted Candy to say "hi" before she entered the store. So she just entered.

Penni began to circle up and down the aisles. Something for him from Freddie and something from Penni. She didn't really care what she got. She didn't care that much about him anyway. She just needed something to cover the dollar amount she was going to keep. However, Freddie might care and so she looked more carefully than she otherwise might have.

Finally Penni found a man's traveling nail kit and a pair of men's travel slippers. That was good. Give him something that says go away for a while. Penni chuckled. Actually they were nice gifts; no one would ever guess the hidden message.

Penni had to time it carefully. Rickles had more customers and you could never tell when a stock boy or the store manager was going to be walking about the store. Penni set her Feldstone bag on the floor between her legs, untwisting the top so it was slightly open as she set it down. Then she picked up a leather case with the slippers inside and appeared to examine it. She kept watching from side to side. The aisle cleared momentarily. She quickly shoved the case into her bag. Then the same with the manicure set. Then Penni picked up another slippers' case and appeared to examine it. She wanted to do one more thing and needed to have an excuse for standing there.

Finally the aisle cleared again. Penni quickly reached down inside the bag and shoved the two items below the robe. Then she closed the bag tightly and strolled over to the check-out. Per usual, Candy's line was longer. By all rights, Penni shouldn't have gotten in it. She hoped it wouldn't look too obvious that she had picked the longest line.

Finally Penni arrived at the cash register. Candy looked down the counter for the check-out items. When she didn't see any she looked up curiously.

"Well, hi Penni!" she said in surprise. "What you doing here?"

"Oh, it's my dad's birthday and I just came by to see if you had anything I wanted to get for him but you didn't."

"Oh, did you see the shaving kits?" Candy asked seriously.

"Yes," said Penni, "but I didn't like them."

"Oh," said Candy. "Then I need to look in your bag."

"Candy!" said Penni in a shocked tone drawing her bag back slightly.

"Oh, it's just something they make us do with anyone," said Candy soothingly. "I just need to see in your bag." She reached for the bag.

"Well, here!" said Penni putting the bag on the counter. "Look, it's a robe my mom is going to give my dad." Before Candy could act, Penni had opened the bag and pulled the robe half way out. "See?" Penni shoved the robe back in the bag. She glanced at the people waiting in line behind her. "Good gracious," she said taking the bag off the counter. "With a long line of customers like this, it's a wonder they'd make you take up your time like that. I'd certainly complain," she said moving by the counter and out into the Mall, "if I were a customer here." She crumpled the top of her bag down tightly and then strode off without looking back.

Major personality changes take place in the alcohlic as alcohol becomes the most important thing in his or her life. The alcoholic will avoid parties or social situations where no alcohol is present. They will hide alcohol "just in case." They will lie if they have to. The thoughts of life without drinking become unbearable. If caught in a situation where the supply has gone dry, a general panic sets in and the alcoholic becomes resourceful enough to usually get alcohol, no matter what. This is how the alcoholic gets the reputation of being a "con artist." Problem drinking adolescents are involved in more antisocial acts, including stealing, than teenagers who are not having problems with alcohol. Teenagers who are recovering from excessive alcohol abuse, will often say they were routinely stealing from their parents during drinking periods. Since many teen alcoholics are also involved in street drugs, becoming a pusher is often the only practical way of maintaining expensive alcohol and drug habits.

Once outside the Mall, Penni let out a long sigh of relief. She couldn't believe it. She had really done it. She had really done it and she hadn't gotten caught. She walked between the parked cars. Once more thing she had to do. She stepped behind a van. Quickly looking around, she tore the price tags off each item. There, that was better. She would have liked to have taken the robe out of the bag and folded it up because it was probably getting wrinkled. But she thought that might look suspicious.

Then Penni went back into the Mall. The money . . . the money . . . it was hers! All that money and it was hers! If she had had any doubts about what she was doing, as soon as she got back in the Mall she forgot them. Now she had to find someone old enough to buy booze. Stupid laws.

It is not hard for teenagers to obtain alcoholic beverages. Some sources are:

1. Buying it oneself in a grocery store or package store. Often retailers will not check ID. If under age and ID will be checked then teenagers use someone else's ID or false IDs ordered through the mail.

Penni—Changes   97

2. *Getting someone of age to purchase the beverage. This can be a regular arrangement with an older friend or it may be a one time situation where an older person is approached on the street to do "a favor."*
3. *Posing as "Of age" in nightclubs and bars. In most towns and cities there are places where it is known that IDs are seldom requested.*
4. *Drinking at home from the parent's supply. Watering down bottles is a common way to cover up this practice.*
5. *Parties in private homes or clubs. Many alcoholics make it a practice to be at parties where alcohol is flowing freely just for the asking.*
6. *Traditional dates where the boy "pays the way" can be a source of alcohol for young females.*
7. *Outright stealing of wine, beer, or liquor from stores, parties, or other people's homes.*

Penni headed for the shoe store. There was a college kid who worked in there who helped out lots of time by buying bottles for them. She saw him watching a customer walk back and forth trying to get the feel of her new shoes.

Penni motioned him over to the door. She knew better than to go in. The store manager didn't like kids hanging around. "Can you buy something for me?" Penni asked.

"No," he said, "I'm working." He seemed a little annoyed.

"I don't mean right now. But when you finish with your customer if another one doesn't come in."

He glanced back at his customer to see if she was through walking and had returned to her seat. She hadn't.

"Please."

"Can't you wait until this evening?"

"No," said Penni. "I gotta have it now." And with that she flashed open her hand with the large supply of cash in it.

He looked surprised as she knew he would. "How much have you got there?"

"Plenty," she answered. "Will you do it?"

"Well," he glanced at the other clerk who was finishing up a customer at the back. "Let me see what happens after this customer goes, huh?"

Penni was surprised he had changed his mind quite so easy but she nodded and moved off. She knew enough not to hang around the shoe store door waiting. She parked herself on the wall space opposite the shoe store and stood there holding her package and idly watching people pass. Occasionally she banged her backside against the wall in a kind of rhythmic anticipation. Wow, was she going to have a good celebration. She smiled to herself.

"Where'd you get all that money?"

Penni started. She hadn't seen the young salesman come out of the store and cross over to her.

"I just got it," she said.

"How much?" he said.

"Enough," she answered again.

"Well," he said. "What do you want? I can only be gone a few minutes."

"I want two bottles," she said.

"Listen, I got something you'll like better than two bottles."

Penni really couldn't imagine that. However, she said, "What is it?"

"C'mon," he said, motioning her to come along with him. She followed him down to a side entrance to the Mall where a store had just closed out. Few people were using the entrance there at this time. He reached into his pocket and pulled out some pills. "I guarantee these will make you feel like you never ever want to come down."

"What are they?"

"Ludes," he said.

"How much?" Penni said.

"Five dollars a pop."

"They are really good, huh?"

"Best I've had all summer. I guarantee it," he said.

Penni felt she could trust him. He wasn't a real runner. But he had good connections and he did enough dealing to know his stuff.

"OK, I'll take two and get me two bottles," Penni said.

"All right," he said. "Wait here. I'll be back."

Penni gave him some of her money. He was back almost before she realized it.

"OK," he said looking around and slipping the bag he carried into her Feldstone's bag. "Listen, come back when you want some more pills."

"Sure," said Penni. "And thanks."

Penni shoved the change he had given her into her pocket. God, she felt rich. Two bottles, some great stuff and money left over. She wondered if she should go back to the main part of the Mall. Maybe she would see some of the kids in the pinball place. No, she decided at last. She really needed to get the booze home safely and she needed to get the robe straightened out. Plus with all the stuff she was taking home, she wouldn't have to go out for anything. If she wanted it, it would be all right by her side at home.

Penni's aunt called out to her as she came in. "Let's see what you got, dear."

"Just a minute," Penni replied. She hurried to her room. Quickly she took the suitcase out from under her bed and loaded the bottles in it. She wanted to take a drink out of the open one that was still in there. However, she also didn't want to delay getting back to her aunt for fear her aunt would come walking in. So instead she put the two new bottles in with the old, quickly closed the lid of the suitcase, and shoved it back under the bed.

Then she took out the other gifts. She put the two things from Rickles in the plain liquor store bag so they would have their own bag. She smoothed out the robe as best she could and slipped it into one of the plain plastics she had gotten when she took the bag. The plastic was a bit big but she folded it under so it looked OK. Then she put it back in the Feldstone bag and took it out to show her aunt.

Penni's aunt seemed quite impressed with the results of her shopping. "I better hide these things away or he might see them," Penni then told her aunt.

"Yes, go do that," she said.

Penni went back to her room. Thank goodness her brother

was still playing with his cousin and was willing to let her hide his present too. She opened her closet door and just dumped the bags on the floor. Hiding them was such a farce. She had made it clear she never wanted her new father to come into her room and he never did.

Penni took out one of the pills. Why not? Why not celebrate? She also took out her old bottle. "Here's to you both," she said, taking the pill with some of her bottle. She put the bottle away while she still knew what she was doing. Then she settled back to enjoy her high. Man, this was worth everything. So now she had stolen, nothing really seemed out of the question. To feel like this she imagined she would do just about anything. It was all so worth it.

Combining any drug with depressant effects and alcohol is dangerous. This practice is like playing Russian roulette because the user never knows when the body will be "put to sleep forever." "Ludes" is a street name for methaqualone (Quaalude ®), a "downer" which in combination with alcohol can cause coma and death. This can be done by taking what might be considered small doses of pills if they were being taken alone. One drug not usually considered a depressant is the hallucinogen, PCP or "angel dust." It slows down vital body functions and its use with alcohol is almost a sure ticket to the emergency room. PCP also has the ability to throw a normal person into a psychotic mental state leading to involuntary admission to a mental hospital for about a month.

---

10 ∾ Jesse—More

Jesse looked down at the check in his hand. He had never held so much money at one time. He still couldn't believe it. He had almost given up on ever getting it. Already he'd been back at school three whole weeks.

It turned out that they had never had any money to pay him all summer long and even when the job had ended, he hadn't been paid. "Red tape," they told him. The money had to come through the Federal regional office and then to the state office and then to the city office and then to his division and it had gotten all fouled up. Jesse didn't understand how programs were funded. He had not understood why they just couldn't pay him. Seemed like all those places had plenty of money. He thought he had just been done out.

But here he was standing in the principal's office with a big check in his hand. Maybe it was better this way. This way he hadn't frittered it away on little things. Now he could get something big.

"What are you going to do with the money?" the principal asked Jesse. "That's quite a nice sum, you know."

"Oh, I know," said Jesse still looking at the check. "I don't really know." He wasn't about to discuss it with the principal anyway.

"Well, Mr. Hinson tells me you were an excellent worker, Jesse. He's really sorry for the delay. You worked hard and you earned it. I hope you put the money to good use."

Jesse thanked the principal. "Is it OK if I fold it?" Jesse had never had a check before and wasn't quite sure how to treat it.

"Sure you can fold it," the principal answered. "Just don't crumple it all up," he added with a smile.

"Oh, no, I won't!" Jesse answered as he carefully folded the check and put it in his pocket.

Jesse wondered as he walked down the street how surprised his mom would be. She was just as sure as he had been when school started that he would never get paid. She'd sure like a new television. Now that she couldn't watch her quiz shows, she didn't have much to do. Wouldn't she be surprised if he came home with a new television. He'd been thinking all along that was what he might do and now he decided that that was it. As a matter of fact he'd buy one on the way home.

Jesse remembered there was a bank over on Trimble Street. He decided to go over there to cash the check. The TV store where they'd bought their last set wasn't too far from that. He quickened his step.

"I'd like to cash this," he said handing his check to the bank teller.

"Do you have an account with us?" she said.

"No ma'am," said Jesse. He and his mother never had enough money to get savings or checking or anything like that. When they had cash, they paid cash. When they didn't have it, they just didn't get.

"I'm sorry," she said. "We don't cash checks that aren't written on our bank unless you have an account with us."

"Well, where can I get it cashed?" he said.

"Well, your check's written on the State Bank, you might try them. There's one four blocks down."

Jesse had never heard of such a thing. What was a bank for unless it was to cash checks.

Jesse swung by the television store. Maybe they would take it directly.

"I'm sorry, sonny," the man said. "We don't cash checks. We just got stung too many times. I'm sure your check is good but we just don't take checks. Look though, I'll hold this television you've picked out until you can come back with the cash. When do you think you can be back?"

"Well, the lady at the other bank said the State Bank would probably cash it since it was written on their bank. So probably today," Jesse said.

Jesse approached the teller at the State Bank. "I'd like to cash this check," he said. "It's from your bank."

The clerk looked at him. It was obvious she didn't see too many teenagers with big checks. "May I see your identification please?" the teller asked.

"Identification?"

"Yes, I can't cash the check without seeing your identification."

"But it's on your bank," he said.

"I know, but we do need your identification."

Jesse reached for his wallet. It was very old and beat up. The only thing in it was a well-worn picture of Jesse with his brother and his social security. "I have my social security card," said Jesse. He had had to get that when he went to work.

"I'm sorry, we can't accept social security cards as ID."

"But it has my name and everything on it," Jesse said.

"I'm sorry. The bank does not consider that valid identification," the clerk said. "I'm sorry. I can't cash the check without identification," she added.

Jesse stood there. He couldn't believe that he had his money but couldn't get it.

"Next please," said the clerk looking around him.

Jesse moved away from the teller's window. What was he going to do?

Jesse walked slowly out of the bank feeling bitter. Here he thought having money made you somebody. And even with money, he had been made to feel just as nothing as before. He kicked a beer bottle on the street corner. But he didn't even bother to turn around and see it skitter and spin. What a fuckin' world this was.

Jesse's mom was home when he got home. He told her what had happened with the check. He hated doing that—it took all of the surprise out of buying her the TV. Well not all the surprise. She still didn't know that was what he was going to do with the money. But now she knew he had the money.

"Look," she finally said. "If you sign the check over to me—first you say 'pay to . . .' and you fill in my name . . . then you sign your name, I bet I can get the lady I used to work for to cash it for me. See, the landlord, he cashes my pension check, 'cause that's how he knows he can get his money. And he gives me the rest. But once and a while if I had to use the money someplace else, I'd get that lady I worked for to cash it for me. That way the landlord didn't get his money till I gave it to him. Here's a pen. You sign it to me."

Jesse hesitated. After the time his mom had got drunk and thrown the bottle at him, she had promised she wouldn't drink any more. If only Jesse had taken that other bottle out of the cupboard right then and there. If only he'd thought to do that, get rid of it. But he hadn't and she'd discovered it and got drunk a couple of times on it. But then she had promised she was on the wagon for good. Jesse didn't know what to do. But he had no choice if he wanted the check cashed.

Jesse pulled out the check. "Here, mom," he said, writing on the back the way she had told him. "When do you think you can do it for me?"

"I'll go by tomorrow, that's what I'll do," said his mother, studying the check. "I'll go by tomorrow." She took the check and put it in her purse.

Jesse went to bed that night dreaming of the television he was going to buy his mom. If she had the money right when he came home from school, he might even have time to go to the television store before it closed. He smiled as he thought about the look she'd get on her face when he brought home the new television.

The next day passed slowly for Jesse. He even thought of cutting his last class at school. Then again, he reasoned, if his mom wasn't home yet, it would just be that much longer to wait. The minute the bell rang, Jesse was out of the door heading for home.

However, the closer he got to home, the more he had an uncomfortable feeling something wasn't right. By the time he got to his house, the feeling was very strong. The smell of booze hit him even as he opened the back door. His mother was sitting at the kitchen table. There was a bottle before her and she had a glass in her hand. There were several bags of groceries sitting around the kitchen but none of the food had been put away.

"Where's my money, mom, did you get it?" Jesse asked.

"Yes," said his mother slightly slurring her words. "I got it," she nodded her head in satisfaction.

The brain controls speech, and when alcohol slows down brain activity, then speech suffers.

In the early stages of alcoholism there is a desire to cut down on the quantity consumed and even attempts to stop completely. Often a person will stop for a specific period of time, say two weeks, to prove to himself, family, and friends that he is not an alcoholic. Holding out for the specified time is often celebrated with a drink which eventually leads to heavy intake again. The inability to stop at one or two drinks is called "Loss of Control."

When brain alcohol levels reach high points, then "blackouts" occur. The intoxicated person may do all sorts of things—some mundane and others quite alarming such as spending all their savings—but is not able to remember anything. Blackouts can be very frightening and sometimes lead a person to recognize they need help.

"Where is the money?"

"Sit down, Jesse," said his mom, "and fix yourself some

sandwich or something. I got lots of groceries. I couldn't even carry them all home. Had to take a taxi."

"Mom, where's my money?" said Jesse more urgently.

"Jesse, sit down, I said, I got some of that new fancy strawberry cake they've been advertising on the radio. Have a piece. Tell me if you like it."

"Mom, I don't want cake. I just want my money. Now give it to me."

"All right," said his mother. She got up swaying slightly. "Now where did I put my purse?" She held onto the kitchen doorway as she moved through to the living room. Jesse followed her. "No, not in here," she said as she looked in the living room. "Now, let's see, what did I do with my purse?" She turned, holding onto the living room doorway and then made her way back to the kitchen.

"Let me see, I paid the cab driver. He brought the groceries in for me. I remember taking the money out and paying him and then I...." She squinted as if trying to picture what she had done. "Oh yes, I remember. I went to the john. That's what I did."

Jesse did not wait for her to move. He turned and walked into the bathroom. There was his mother's purse in the middle of the floor. He picked it up and tore it open. Her wallet was open inside the purse but there was only small change in it—no bills. He quickly sorted through the other junk she carried in her purse but there was no money there.

Jesse stalked back to the kitchen. "Mom," he said. "The money's not in there!"

"But it must be," said his mother. She was sitting down at the table again. "Here, let me see that." As she reached for the purse, she knocked her glass over and the dark brown smelly stuff ran all over the table. "Oh damn," she said. Without bothering to wipe it up she took the bottle and poured herself another drink. She took a drink out of the glass and then held the rim slightly below the edge of the table. With her hand she tried to bring some of the runny liquid to the edge of the table and then into her glass. But she succeeded mostly in pushing it either into her lap or onto the floor. "It's wet stuff, isn't it?" she said looking at her hand and then taking a lick from it. "Good to the last drop." She raised her glass and took another drink.

"Mom!" Jesse shouted. "It's gone. My money, it's gone, where is it?"

"Well, if it's not in there, Jesse," his mother said with a shrug of resignation, "I don't know where it is 'cause that's where I put it and that's where it was."

"Mom," said Jesse, "try to think. What did you do after you got the money?"

"Well, let's see. I thought I'd celebrate getting your money by stopping in at the Red Lion. After all, I had washed all those glasses and I thought I might just as well have a drink out of one and see if indeed they had changed their drinks. And then after I had some drinks there, I remember I went to the drug store and bought one of those hair blowers I'd been wanting. Then I thought I better buy you some groceries so I did that and then I took the cab and came straight home."

"Try to remember, mom. When you paid the cab driver, how much money did you have in your purse?"

"Why, just the right amount of dollars, I remember. He said it was four dollars and that's just exactly what I had. Glad it wasn't any more 'cause I wouldn't have known what to pay him with."

"But, mom, you didn't buy near enough stuff to have spent all the money. What did you do with the rest of it?"

"Look, Jess, I told you everything I know. I told you I got the money. I told you where I went and what I got. Now the rest is up to you to figure out. I told you all I know. I can't tell you any more." His mother took another big swallow from her glass.

Jesse stood looking at her trying to fight back the tears. "Oh mom, you lost my money."

"I didn't lose it, Jess," his mother said. "I told you I put it in my purse and that's where it is and if it's not there then I don't know where it is because that's where I put it." She put her glass down on the table with a thud to emphasize the point and then she picked up the bottle and filled the glass again.

Jesse stood looking at her, searching for words. Then suddenly he wheeled around and stormed out of the house. "Damn it," he cried as he strode quickly out to the street. "God damn it, mother, how could you have? How could you have?"

Jesse started to run. He didn't know where he was going. He just started to run. All the while he was saying, "Damn it, damn it! Mother, how could you have? How could you?" He vaguely remembered running down past Ollie's store and a block or two more before he stopped to catch his breath. He didn't know whether to run some more or what. He wished the ground would start to crumble and he would find himself falling through with earth and rocks tumbling in after him. Oh, God, he thought.

Finally through the muddle in his mind, he heard a voice calling to him. "Jesse, Jesse, c'mon over." It was the guys he had gotten so drunk with early in the summer. He crossed the street. One pulled out a bag with a bottle in it. "Want some?"

This time Jesse didn't hesitate. "Sure," he said. "That's exactly what I want." He raised the bag to his lips and took a long drink. He paused and looked down at the boy who had offered it to him. "That's exactly what I want." He took another long drink. Then he wiped his mouth and handed it back. "Thanks," he said. "Wish I had something to return the favor. But," he said with a twisted smile. "I just happen to be broke right now."

"That's all right," said the guy. "I'll stand you one more time."

"Do you. . . ?" Another boy started to ask Jesse something. However, they were interrupted by a car careening down the street. Just as the previous times, the occupants were hanging out the window yelling insults at them.

"What we need," said the other boy, "is to get some cash

and get us one of them things and do that right back to them all the length of this God damn city."

"Yeah," said another boy. "But just when and where are we going to get that kind of cash?"

"There are ways and there are places," said the other boy. "Pass me that," he said motioning to the bag, "and maybe I'll tell you about some."

Jesse shared the bottle another time and listened as they began to talk of the money just sitting around waiting for somebody to do a little "polite asking." When one of the boys said the word *polite*, he patted the pocket of his jacket. Jesse wasn't sure what he meant. But he saw the boy had something in his pocket.

The bottle went around another couple of times. Finally one of the boys said, "Let's do it. Let's do some asking. If you don't ask, how you ever going to get."

Jesse's head was swimming. He wondered if it was because he had been running and his heart had been pumping so fast the alcohol had gotten in his blood much sooner. He didn't feel sick like last time but he knew he was already not himself.

"C'mon guys," one boy said and they put their arms around each other and started off.

Jesse walked along with them as best he could. Once or twice he shook his head trying to clear it. It really was hard to concentrate on what they were talking about.

Finally Jesse saw the light of Ollie's store coming up on the left. The boys turned to go in. Jesse felt like he needed cool air—not the warm air of a store.

"Not me," he said. "I've gotta stay in the fresh air." He walked over to the street light which had just come on and leaned against it. The street twirled a little. He felt himself grab onto the light to steady himself. He tried focusing his eyes on the car parked out front.

Suddenly he heard shots and someone screaming. He blinked and turned back toward the store. He saw his friends run out of the store and start going in all directions. Then he saw Ollie come out. But Ollie wasn't walking right.

Then through his haze he saw Ollie fall. Something red ran out from under Ollie's white apron. Jesse stared and then he sank to his knees and began to sob. "They've shot Ollie. My God, they've shot Ollie. Those kids shot Ollie. Oh no. Oh no."

Suddenly he felt a firm hand on his shoulder and a voice calling, "Jesse. Jesse, c'mon kid get up. It's OK. C'mon Jesse."

But Jesse could only moan. "They shot Ollie. They shot Ollie."

"C'mon Jesse." The voice was insistent.

Jesse kept thinking there was something familiar about that voice.

"C'mon Jess," the voice was quiet and insisting. "C'mon Jesse."

Suddenly Jesse remembered. He looked up quickly. It was Tom! Tom standing there in his army uniform calling to him.

"Tom!" Jesse staggered to his feet and threw his arms around his brother. "Tom," Jesse sobbed. "They shot Ollie."

"I know Jesse, I know," was all Jesse remembered Tom's saying and then he passed out.

Alcohol does not "cause" people to engage in criminal behavior but drinking does contribute to the overall poor judgement and lack of control involved in crime. Many people arrested for crimes are intoxicated and many victims are taken advantage of in an intoxicated state. In one study, over seventy percent of robbery offenders were involved with alcohol. In another study of murder cases, eighty-six percent of the offenders had been drinking.

---

11 ~ Christine—More

Christine looked in the liquor cabinet. She had to find a bottle that was open but didn't have so much gone it would be obvious if she took some. She selected the vodka. I'll just mix it with orange juice, she thought.

Christine took the bottle to the kitchen, got a glass of orange juice and poured in a healthy amount of vodka, then put the bottle back. She looked at the Scotch bottle as she did. It was almost empty. She had some of that last week and replaced what she took with water. Aparently no one had noticed.

She looked at the clock. Her mother wouldn't be home for at least another hour. What an icky day. She'd gotten her test back from last week. The teacher had written across it: "Christine, what's the matter with you?" It had been that way ever since school started—teachers getting on her back about her work. No, it had been that way even at the end of the summer. Her dance teacher had told her that unless her performance improved, she might not be able to be in the dance recital. And her swim coach had pulled her from the last two matches saying she just wasn't swimming right. That had made her feel really stupid when the team won the overall championship and she had had to stand up with the rest of them for the medals—even though she hadn't swum in almost a fourth of the meets.

Why was everyone bugging her? Her mother had even said that unless she showed some improvement at school, she wouldn't be able to go out Saturday. Christine frowned. School was such a bore. Saturday night was just about the most important thing in the world. Well, she'd have to ditch her test paper so her parents wouldn't see it.

Christine took another sip of her drink and leaned back against the couch. Saturday. It was going to be fantastic. Herbert—that was a terrible name but if he could put up with it, she could—was going to take her to the basketball game. She had decided not to be a cheer leader this year. If you were a cheer leader you never got to go and sit with a boy and since she had met Herbert, she didn't want to be down front anymore.

Actually, she hadn't just met Herbert—she had been fixed up by, of all people, Mark Geigy. She guessed Arthur had said some nice things or else Mark had thought she was nice. Anyway he had fixed her up with Herbert, this other senior, only a week or two after Arthur left. Even though they went most of the places Mark and Sandra went, Herbert had his own car so there was no problem of driving with Mark.

Herbert was eighteen so he could legally drink and no one ever questioned her when she was with him. Lots of times after games, they'd stop some place and have something to drink. Most often, however, they drank in someone's home; sometimes at parties where parents provided drinks. More often when the parents were out, they just brought liquor into someone's home.

Christine was surprised how quickly drinking had become part of her life. But it wasn't "drinking" like something she did way out there in isolation. Drinking was just part of the whole dating thing—what the kids did. It made them feel very grown up and they had some riotous times. Remembering how sick and dizzy she had been after drinking the first time, Christine tried to avoid its happening again. The trick, she discovered, was to drink enough to feel up and free enough to have a great time but to stop just before it pushed her over into feeling woosey so that she didn't have a good time. "Drinking to the edge" she called it. Sometimes she knew if she took one more sip, it would push her over. Sometimes she misjudged and got dizzy anyway. However, that was less and less. She seemed to be able to judge better.

Only once did Christine get really vomiting sick. That was so embarrassing she could have died. However, Herbert had continued to ask her out. She adored going with the senior crowd. All her old friends including her best friend, Kay, seemed so immature or something. It was just like she'd grown up all of a sudden and left them behind.

She'd even gotten into a fight with Kay. "Christine, what's the matter with you? You're not like you used to be at all," Kay had complained. "We used to be friends. Now you're running off with Sandra and those guys all the time."

"Well you're just jealous. You just wish you could go with a senior too," Christine had retorted, stung by her friend's criticism.

"No, I don't," Kay had snapped back. "Not if it would do to me what it's doing to you."

"What's it doing to me?" Christine had said coldly.

"Well, you're different. You don't seem to care about things anymore. You're just not a friend."

"I'm still your friend, Kay. Apparently you're not mine," Christine had replied and then turned and walked off.

The only real problem Christine felt she had was with Herbert. The kids made out a lot. She and Herbert did too simply because there were times that that was all there was to do. He had been pressuring her to go further and further. Christine didn't like Herbert that much. However, she was afraid he'd stop asking her out if she didn't go further each time. Herbert was her ticket to the senior group right now. Maybe through him she could get to know someone she'd really like.

Christine sipped her drink thoughtfully. Already she was beginning to feel better about her test. She could do the work if she wanted to, she knew that. She had been practically a straight A student last year. It was just that she didn't want to. I mean it just wasn't all that important.

Alcoholism is a progressive illness. That means that alcohol becomes a preoccupation and finally affects every aspect of an individual's life. Twenty-five things to watch for in becoming alcoholic include:
1. *Mood swings*
2. *Sneaking drinks*
3. *Stealing to obtain drinking money*
4. *Drop in grades*
5. *Missing what a teacher is saying because of being "high" or "groggy"*
6. *Being absent from school because of drinking*
7. *Drinking alone*
8. *Drinking in the morning before school*
9. *Gulping drinks*
10. *Inability to predict how much you will drink before you start*
11. *Drinking when angry or when you have difficult problems to face*
12. *Health problems*
13. *Parents and/or friends angry about drinking*
14. *Forgetting what happened while drinking*
15. *Arrested while drinking*
16. *Worrying about drinking*
17. *Feeling guilty about drinking*
18. *Avoiding old and possible new friends who do not drink*
19. *Planning days so that alcohol will be available*
20. *Getting angry when someone tries to talk to you about drinking*
21. *Loss of interest in hobbies or other activities which used to take up a lot of time*
22. *Hiding alcohol*
23. *Feeling sick (nausea, shaking, headache, insomnia, seeing things that are not there, etc.) when trying to stop*
24. *A change in concern for appearance*
25. *Feeling a hundred percent better after a drink*

Christine took another sip. Then she heard the car motor in the drive. Golly, was that her mother home already? She couldn't believe it. The time had gone so fast. Christine finished off the drink and then took out a breath mint and popped it in her mouth.

"Hi, mom," she called gaily when her mother entered the door.

"Hi, Christine. My goodness, you're cheerful."

"That's me, cheery Christine," Christine called. "You know that."

"Well, actually Christine, I don't know that. You've been so moody lately. One minute you're flying high and the next minute you're down in the dumps. I can't keep track of you. At any rate, I'm glad you're feeling good right now."

"Can I help you with anything?" Christine was off the couch. She padded into the kitchen in her bare feet and put her glass in the sink.

"What was that you were having dear?" her mother asked, noticing the glass.

"Orange juice," said Christine. "Got to get my vitamin C or I'll get scurvy and I just want to be curvy, not scurvy," she said, giving her mother a kiss on the cheek.

Her mother gave her an odd glance. "Well, Miss Curvy, how did you do on your test last week? Those grades you've been bringing home have been pretty terrible."

"Oh Miss Carter said I did fine. I don't have my test back yet because she had some kind of problem with something or other and she said she didn't have time to enter the grades in the book even though she had graded them. But I asked her about mine and she told me."

Christine was surprised how smoothly the lie came out. She never used to lie to her parents at all. Now it seemed she was constantly lying. It still bothered her but not all that much. Life just seemed to go so much smoother when she told her parents what they wanted to hear rather than what she wanted to say.

Most people tell "white" lies at times to protect themselves from embarrassment or to justify something done. In the alcoholic, this practice becomes exaggerated to rationalize to himself and others his unusual preoccupation with drinking. Since family members, teachers, and friends do not want to believe someone close to them is ill, they tend to accept feeble rationalizations time and time again. This is one reason why alcoholism is a social and family disease. Soon the sick person is in a web of denial about what is really happening. "So I drink a little—everyone does." "I can't get going this morning, I must be coming down with the flu." "I'll take a little bit of dad's booze just to get me going—he will never miss it." What seems to others like straight out lying is really a projection outward of the alcoholic's fantasy world. It's a symptom of the disease.

"Well, I'm glad dear" her mother said. "I've been worried about you. You just seem so changed all of a sudden. I mean, not wanting to try out for cheer leading this year, and not doing well in school. I wonder if this boy you're running around with isn't having a bad influence on you."

"Oh mother, we've been over that. Herbert is just a nice guy. I'm not in love with him or anything. We just go out and have a good time, that's all."

"Well it's not always clear where you go on these dates. And I really don't approve of your coming home as late as you have been now that the school year has started. It was one thing during the summer but it's school time now."

Christine had a warm feeling spreading inside her. The alcohol made her care less about her mother's criticism than she would have done had she been sober. "Oh mother," she said. "You worry too much. You certainly don't want to go putting restraints on me just as I may be needing a bit of freedom." There was something familiar about those words that struck both Christine and her mother.

"Christine, have you been listening in on your father's and my conversations?"

"I don't think so, mom," said Christine innocently. "We sit at the dinner table and whenever you and dad start to talk I immediately close my ears so I won't hear."

"Christine," said her mother laughing. "Sometimes I don't know what to make of you these days."

"Make of me what you will," said Christine giving a low

bow, "but just say I can go to Loretta Banks' birthday party Saturday night."

"Well, since you got a good grade on your test, I guess I can't say no," said her mother. "What kind of a birthday party is this Loretta Banks having? I don't think I know her."

"Oh I don't know her either really," said Christine. "She's a friend of Mark and Sandra's and Herbert and I are going. See, Saturday, we're playing Lakewood and she goes to Lakewood and since we'll be over at Lakewood after the game, she's invited us to her party."

"Well, that's very nice of her since she doesn't know you."

"Well, she knows Mark though, see."

"Yes, I guess so," said Christine's mother. "But I want you to leave that party early enough to be home at a reasonable time. And since Lakewood is in the next township, you're going to have to take driving time into consideration."

"Oh we will, mother. A birthday party can't last all that long and since we don't know her, we'll probably stop in just for a little while. Listen, I've got to go wash my hair if it's going to look right tomorrow. If you don't need any help, I'll go do it now."

"No," said her mother, "I'm just fixing a very simple dinner. You go wash your hair. When you come down you can set the table."

"Okey-Dokey, Dokey, Dokey . . ." said Christine doing a twirl and walking out of the kitchen with an exaggerated hip movement.

Her mother looked after her with a puzzled expression.

Christine made her way back from the bathroom to where Herbert was sitting. There were kids sprawled all over so she had to be careful where she stepped. The smoke made the room blue in the dim light and the noise was really something.

"I can't believe this party," she said when she reached Herbert. "I've never seen so much booze and grass."

"Yeah," said Herbert, "maybe we do go to the wrong school."

"After that game, I can believe it," Christine added. "What a terrible score."

"Wanna puff?" Someone passed Herbert a reefer.

"Thanks," said Herbert taking a drag and passing it to Christine.

"No thanks," said Christine. She passed it on.

"What's a matter, you don't ever take them?" Herbert said.

"It ruins the booze," said Christine.

Herbert paused and thought. "Yeah, you're right, but it ruins it so beautifully."

"Hey," he said, taking her hand and pulling her up with him. "Bring your glass. Let's move out of here, this noise is getting to me."

He led Christine to one of the rooms where jackets and coats had been piled on the bed. Christine felt foggy as she moved into the room with him. The smoke and the booze seemed to be getting to her.

Herbert shoved some coats off the bed onto the floor. "C'mon sit down here," he said patting the bed. He filled her glass from the bottle he had brought along with them. Christine was not sure whether or not she should drink anymore but drinking might keep Herbert away so she sat and drank.

The next thing Christine remembered was like coming up from a well. Herbert was lying on top of her and he had pulled her pants down.

"No," Christine said, but she felt very uncoordinated and groggy. Herbert was kissing her. She hated the way he was doing it. It was very animal like. "No," she said trying to move out from under him. "No," said Christine again. "Don't."

"C'mon," said Herbert. "You did it with Mark's other friend, so why not me?"

"I did not!" said Christine.

"Oh c'mon," said Herbert. "Mark told me all about it. A little horseback ride and a nice roll in the grass."

"That's a lie," said Christine pushing at him. She felt his penis touching her pubic hair. She panicked. What if

I can't stop him? She felt him getting closer to entering her.

"Oh no," she said out loud trying to worm out from under him. But the more she struggled the more determined he seemed.

"You bitch! Why do you think I've been dating you, for all these weeks? Now come across!"

"Get off me," said Christine. "You disgust me."

"Well, see if this disgusts you," he grunted thrusting into her.

Christine felt exhausted and as if she had lost. But she made one final effort. The coats they were lying on moved. Then suddenly they gave way sending them both cascading down onto the floor.

Christine scrambled up, pulling up her pants. It was then that she became aware a bunch of kids had been watching them from the doorway. They had amused looks on their faces. Christine pushed past them out into the other room. She had to find Sandra and Mark. They were nowhere to be seen. She searched the main party room again. Where could they be?

Christine sat on a hardback chair in a corner by herself, looking across the room. She wanted to go home. She didn't dare call her parents though. She'd never be able to explain if they had to come all the way to Lakewood to get her. They'd never let her go out again. Where were Sandra and Mark?

Christine saw Herbert re-enter the room. He didn't look for her at all. Instead he sat down with a group of kids on some pillows in the center and started to drink again. Oh where were Sandra and Mark?

After what seemed to be a long time, she saw Sandra and Mark coming down from upstairs. Mark had his arm around Sandra and she was resting her head on his shoulder. They came slowly down the stairs. Christine fairly leaped out of her chair.

"Let's go," she begged as soon as she saw them.

"Why?" said Sandra. "Where's Herbert?"

"He's over there," said Christine nodding at the people sitting on the pillows.

"Wanna go, Sandra?" asked Mark.

"I don't know. I suppose we could. It doesn't really matter to me," and she gave him a kiss on his cheek.

"Well, let's see what Herbert says," said Mark. He left the two girls standing together and went over to Herbert.

Christine could see them talking together. Mark looked back at Christine once.

"Yeah," said Mark when he arrived back where Christine and Sandra waited. "He says he's ready to go. I told him to bring the coats. I wasn't going to fight my way through that mob one more time."

They started out the door. Christine didn't look back to see if Herbert was coming till they were outside by the cars.

"Geez, it's cold," said Mark unlocking his car door. He helped Sandra into his car. Then he got in and started the car motor to get his car warm. Mark was laughing and joking and was obviously feeling very good.

Christine stood freezing by Herbert's car. After what seemed like an interminable amount of time, Herbert appeared carrying all their coats. He passed Sandra's and Mark's through their windows to them. Then he handed Christine her coat without even looking at her. He went around to the other side of the car leaving her to struggle into her coat by herself. Herbert let himself in and then reached over and unlocked her door. He let her open it and get in.

Herbert started the motor and switched on the headlights. His head turned to back out. He said nothing to Christine. Christine sat in the darkened car feeling very cold and very alone. Mark had already started down the street. Herbert accelerated to keep up with him.

Christine pressed back in her seat. She didn't know whether it was standing in the cold or the whole experience but suddenly Christine felt very sober. God, what is happening to me, she thought. Here I am riding along with this guy I don't even like very well. I've almost just been raped by him and I don't even like the way he kisses. My best friend, Kay, has told me she thinks I'm bonkers. I lie to my parents. I'm not doing any of the things I like to do. I skip dance practice.

Christine—More

I'm not a cheer leader. My teachers think I'm crazy or stupid this year. What is going on with me?

Suddenly Christine saw herself in a new light. All at once she saw the "new" Christine and she didn't like her very much at all.

"Bastard." The swerve of the car and the sound of Herbert's voice brought Christine out of her trance. Christine looked back. A slow moving car was rapidly disappearing behind them.

Christine turned around. It was then she became aware of how fast they were going and how much the car ahead of them was weaving on the road. She glanced at the speedometer. They were fifteen miles above the speed limit. However, Herbert seemed to be holding his car much steadier than Mark was doing with his.

Depending upon one's weight, one or at most two drinks rarely affect responsible driving. Beyond that, the probability of being seriously affected becomes much greater. The following table* shows the affects of number of drinks on responsible driving:

Wt.	Drinks Two-Hour Period 1½ ozs 86° Liquor or 12 ozs. Beer
100	1 2 3 4 5 6 7 8 9 10 11 12
120	1 2 3 4 5 6 7 8 9 10 11 12
140	1 2 3 4 5 6 7 8 9 10 11 12
160	1 2 3 4 5 6 7 8 9 10 11 12
180	1 2 3 4 5 6 7 8 9 10 11 12
200	1 2 3 4 5 6 7 8 9 10 11 12
220	1 2 3 4 5 6 7 8 9 10 11 12
240	1 2 3 4 5 6 7 8 9 10 11 12

Be Careful
BAC to .05

Driving Impaired
.05—.09

Do Not Drive
.10 & Up

*Table prepared by National Highway Traffic Safety Administration

Christine automatically gripped the side of her seat as they swerved around the corner. She glanced over at Herbert's face which was lit only by the light of the dashboard. It was tense and angry. Christine wanted to say something to him about the way Mark and Sandra's car was wobbling back and forth on the road.

Suddenly she saw Mark's car swerve, then veer off the road. It seemed to sideswipe a telephone pole. The doors flew open. Christine screamed as the car smashed into a tree. She turned her head as Herbert desperately tried to bring his car to a stop.

Herbert's car gradually bumped to a halt. Christine got out and ran back sobbing toward the accident. She could hear the horn blowing on Mark's car. Porch lights were coming on in the nearby houses and people were coming out. Christine stumbled on the grass, caught her balance and kept on running. When she got to the car, she pushed through the crowd of people. Mark was pinned behind the wheel, his head tossed back. His mouth was open and there was blood running out of it. There didn't appear to be anyone on the seat next to him.

Driving accidents are the number one cause of violent death in the United States. One-third of traffic injuries and one-half of traffic fatalities are alcohol related. In most states, driving with an alcohol level of .10 percent or more is illegal. Police may stop a driver at any time if there are signs of impaired driving. When one applies for and receives a driver's license, one is giving permission to submit to an alcohol breath test if judged to be needed by a policeman.

Christine started to run around to the other side of the car. However, not far from the wreck she saw another group of people. Two of them were kneeling on the ground beside someone. "Sandra," Christine sobbed and ran toward the group of people. Someone moved back to let her in. Christine gasped. Sandra's one eye was partly out and the side of her face was covered with blood.

"Oh, Sandra," Christine said and had to be held from trying to take her in her arms.

"She's still alive. The ambulance is on its way," someone said. "C'mon over here."

"Sandra," Christine called out over her shoulder as someone forcibly made her walk away.

She didn't want to walk away with these strangers. She wanted to stay with her friend. "Sandra, Sandra," she kept sobbing. The horn's loud ugly sound went on. There were voices everywhere and eventually sirens.

Later that night Christine lay in bed. Her mind alternately raced rapidly and then went numb. However, she couldn't seem to shut the sound out of her ears. Even though it wasn't there, she continued to hear Mark's horn blasting on and on and on. Christine rolled over and tried to muffle the sound with her pillow. But the sound went on and on.

Suddenly she felt her mother's soft hands on her back. "There, dear, it's all right."

"Oh, mom," Christine cried turning over and throwing herself into her mother's arms. "The horn, the horn, I can still hear the horn."

"I know dear," her mother said, cradling Christine's head against her body.

"Mother," Christine sobbed. She wanted to pour out everything, about how she had been acting and what had been going on in her life. But she couldn't. Instead, she could only say. "Mother, oh mother."

Her mother patted her head. "There, there, Christine," she said. "There, there."

Slowly the beating of her mother's heart became louder than the horn. Christine felt her body begin to relax. "Oh mother," she said once again in a quiet sorrow.

"I'm here, Christine. I'm here," her mother said.

Christine remembered her mother's saying that when she was a little girl and afraid of the dark. Christine felt her body get heavy. Her eyes closed. "I don't want to be grown up," murmured Christine in a near sleep. "Please don't let me be grown up. Please don't."

12 ~ Penni—More

Penni stared down at the suitcase. She was beginning to shake a little. She really needed to have a drink. But the fact was the bottle in the suitcase was empty. Her mind whirled trying to put it all together. She never would have let this happen. As a matter of fact, she knew she hadn't let it happen. She had learned there were times when she had to have a drink so she always got another bottle before the one at home ran out.

At first she had thought she just was so high she wasn't keeping good track and that was why her bottles seemed to be getting emptier sooner. But also sometimes it tasted funny like it had water in it. She had had to drink more to feel good so the booze really went fast. Finally she had really started to watch. And with every week she got surer something was wrong.

Now she knew for sure. Someone had been into her booze. And there was only one person it could be. Her brother! If either her mom or her dad had found the stuff, they would have called her on it right away. But her brother! It had to be him!

At first she couldn't believe it. What would a little kid like that want with booze? Jesus, he was much too young to drink.

Although she didn't have all that much to do with him, Penni really liked her brother. The thought of his drinking didn't appeal to her.

The age when young people are taking their first drink and using other drugs is lowering. Some reports indicate many preteens are experimenting with alcohol and some are already heavy drinkers. Studies are now underway to determine the long-term effects of alcohol and drug use by preteens—both physiologically and psychologically. Probably the greatest danger is an early learned dependence on alcohol and drugs to escape normal stresses and therefore an inability to develop normal coping ability.

Penni realized she now had a major problem. First of all she had enough trouble supporting her own need for booze let alone someone else's. But more important if her brother drank, her parents were going to find out about her for sure. Her brother was too little and not clever enough to keep on hiding the fact that he was drinking. Why, he wasn't even clever enough to leave a little bit in her bottle.

God what a terrible turn of events. How could he? How could that little kid get hooked on booze? And how did he find out about hers? Penni was sick inside. Plus she began to feel dizzy. If she had needed a drink before, now she really needed a drink.

Penni slammed the lid on the suitcase shut and shoved it under the bed. Penni had sneaked out of school early to get home to her booze. Now what was she to do? She went into her parents' bedroom. She pulled open the dresser drawer. Sometimes she had found some money there. No luck. She hurriedly opened the closet door. Maybe in her dad's pants pockets, or her mother's coat pocket. No luck. She looked over toward her mother's jewelry box. But selling a piece of jewelry might take days. She had found that out with the one piece she had already taken. And she needed a drink now.

Where could she get some money? Her mind raced. Nowhere, damn it, nowhere. She thought of going to the Mall and trying to steal the wallet out of someone's purse. But she knew she would be no good at that. Merchandise she could steal but not something someone was hanging on to. And a kid out of school at this time of day would be a sitting duck in a liquor store.

No, she had to get the money. But she couldn't get the money. So what. She had to get a bottle. Suddenly something clicked in her mind. Last week, they'd gotten some mail that didn't belong to them. Penni had taken it up to the couple on the fourth floor and when they'd opened the door, she remembered seeing that they had a beautiful bar in their apartment. There had been bottles—the fancy crystal kind—sitting on it. But how to get in? There was an old lady on the third floor who was home every day. She'd have to be quiet. How to get in? She knew the apartments in their building. There was no way to budge the door lock.

Penni started shaking again. Her mind raced. She had to have something to drink. What about the windows? She walked over to the front window of their own apartment and looked up. Her heart sank. There was no way to get in. The sides of the building were smooth. This was a fireproof building and there were no fire escapes on the outside. There was no way to get in. Penni stared out at the street. The janitor for the apartment complex was down front with a hose washing down the sidewalk.

Penni started. Of course. She had it! She tucked the apartment key she carried on a ribbon around her neck inside her blouse. Then she ran out of her apartment and down to the street level. Noting the janitor's back was turned, she darted out of the building front door onto the sidewalk behind him.

"Hello," she said.

He turned. "Look at this mess. You tell people to curb their dogs and what do they do? Let 'em go right in the middle of the sidewalk. I stepped right in it. Look," he turned his foot sideways so Penni could see the brown smut that caked the arch, heel, and back side of his shoe.

"Yic," said Penni.

"I want to get it hosed off before the kids start coming home from school. Hey," he said, looking more closely at her. "Aren't you supposed to be in school?"

"Yes," said Penni and she shook a little. "But I don't feel well and so they sent me home to lie down. Trouble is, I don't have a key. Can you let me have yours so I can get in?"

"I'm not supposed to give anyone the master key," he said turning back to his hose. "I'll let you in just as soon as I finish this."

"Well, I really don't feel well. I'd like to go in and lie down now."

"Well then," he said a little annoyed. "Let me shut off the water and I'll go up and let you in."

"Oh," said Penni, "but then you'll get dog do all over the hall carpets and have to clean it up afterwards." Penni knew how much their janitor hated extra work, particularly cleaning the halls. He'd complained about it often enough. "Really," Penni said sweetly, "just give me the key. I'll go right up and open the door and bring it right back."

"Well," said the janitor. "Well, OK if you're sick." He reached into his pocket and pulled out a ring of keys. "It's this one," he said flipping them over and handing them to her with the master key on top.

"I'll be right back," said Penni. She moved slowly up the walkway to the door like she was ill. However, her mind was racing. She had to make it up to the fourth floor and back in the time it would take to go to the second floor where she lived.

The minute she was inside she bolted up the steps. She reached the fourth floor and her heart was pounding. She shoved the key in the lock and turned the handle. It wouldn't go. She turned the key furiously and shoved against the handle. The door opened. She yanked the key out of the lock, pulled the door to her so it was almost closed. Then she bolted back down the stairs and out the front door.

"Here you are," she said trying to control her breathing.

"Thanks," said the janitor glancing down at her and taking

the keys. Suddenly he said, "Hey, I thought you said you didn't have a key."

Penni looked down. Her key was hanging out in front of her blouse. It must have jounced out when she ran up and down the stairs. She swallowed.

"That's why I'm a little out of breath," she said. "I left it at home this morning and I ran into my room to get it before I came down. It would be just like me to bring you back the keys and lock myself out and have to come back to get them."

"Oh," said the janitor. "Well, remember to wear it next time. I might not be here if you need to get in."

"Oh, I will," said Penni. "And thanks." She turned and walked slowly back into the building. Once inside she gave a sigh of relief and climbed carefully to the top floor. She walked over to the door she had just unlocked and cautiously opened it. She knew no one was there. They both worked and they were never there until about six. Still, she felt a little funny going in.

Her body was now very shaky. She had to have a drink. She hurried to the bar. Each bottle had a little silver tag around its neck, like a little dog collar. She read them quickly: bourbon, gin, Scotch. Scotch—that would do it pretty fast. She took out the glass stopper. Without looking for a glass she raised the decanter to her lips and drank until she needed to get her breath. Then she paused, took a breath, and then drank again. Some of the brown liquid spilled out on her chin and ran down on her blouse. She didn't care. This was what she needed.

Penni held the decanter in her hand while a quiet warm peacefulness took over her body. Then she took another long drink. Finally she set the bottle and the stopper down on the counter. Geez, they had a lot of booze. She slipped back the sliding door underneath the bar. There was a replacement bottle for each of those above. Momentarily she thought of just taking a bottle. But they kept things so neat, they would know. So if they knew, what would they know? Better not to take a chance. Why hadn't she thought to bring her own bottle to fill? Maybe she could find a container in the kitchen.

Penni walked into the kitchen. The apartment was on the opposite side of the hall from what hers was so the layout was the same but flipped over. That gave her a weird sense of having been there, but not having been there. She looked around—what could she use? She opened the cabinet underneath the sink. Maybe something in there. Sure enough, she pulled a soft drink bottle out from among the cigarette butts in the garbage. She could use this.

Penni rinsed the bottle off lightly under the sink water. Then she walked back into the living room. Better not take the Scotch. She had had a lot of that already. I guess I'll take the bourbon. Gin tastes like stale perfume.

She took off the stopper and began to pour it slowly into the coke bottle. Some bourbon spilled on the bar. "Damn," she said. She hated to waste it. Plus, she'd have to wipe it up. Oh well, here goes. She began to pour faster. To her surprise it worked better. She filled the coke bottle half way. The bourbon container was beginning to look a little empty. Well she needed it more than they did.

Penni filled the coke bottle three-quarters of the way full. She set the container down. She better not take any more. She went back to the kitchen. "Where's the paper towels," she mumbled half out loud. She found some over the counter and went back in and wiped up the bar. She straightened up the bottles and put them on the bar as she had found them. Then she took the towels back out to the kitchen and stuffed them into the garbage can under the cigarettes and trash. "Yic," she got ashes on her hand. She rinsed her hands off at the sink and then wiped them off on her skirt.

Penni closed the cabinet door under the sink and looked around the kitchen. Everything was just as she had found it except for the soft drink bottle of booze on the counter. She was ready to go. She took the bottle and started into the living room.

Just then the door to the apartment flew open and three policemen, guns drawn, rushed in.

"Freeze!" one yelled pointing his gun at her. "You're under arrest!"

13 ∾ Jesse—Choices

Jesse sat in the waiting room with Tom. "You sure this is the way you want it?" said Tom.

Jesse looked down at the floor. He tried to think about it one more time. Ever since Tom had talked to him, he had been thinking about it.

A nurse came by. "The doctor will be with you in just a minute," she said.

Jesse glanced up and then back at the floor.

"It's this way," Tom had said. "I saved all my Army pay. I brought it home to you and mom. But how it's spent is going to be your choice. You can decide. I'm either going to give it to you so you can get out of here—go someplace nice, maybe send you to a special high school where you can learn something so you can start doing something with yourself. Or I'm going to send mom to a treatment program. I can't do both. I learned a lot in the Army about how they help guys who start drinking too much. They got treatment programs for them. Sometimes it works real good."

Jesse's mind had whirled. Maybe he could get out, get out like Tom had gotten out. Go to a special training school. Get a chance to get a fine job. *Be somebody.*

Jesse—Choices

"I'd work hard," Jesse said. "I'd really try."

"I know," said Tom. "You could do it. I know you could. The guy who told me about this special school place said a buddy of his went and now this buddy was working for some big company and he drives a great car and travels all over the west doing stuff."

"But don't you have to be somebody special to go?"

"Naw, they take you on what's called 'aptitude'—means if you can pass the test, they'll let you in. You not only get to get your high school diploma but you get this other training besides."

"Do you think I could pass the test?" Jesse had said.

"Of course, you can pass the test. I've seen the stuff you can do. And I know you can do it. You've got real ability for that stuff."

"Before I went overseas this friend, he took me by this place and I talked to the man who runs it. He told me how much I would have to have to send you there. I've got that now. My buddy's mom and dad would let you stay with them free. And I'd just give you the money you need for meals and stuff. Pretty town. Real pretty town. Kinda quiet. But real pretty town. Nice place to be doing it, you know what I mean?"

Jesse nodded. He could picture white houses and neat lawns and trees and this school where you got this special training. "I'd work hard," Jesse had said.

Tom said, "You don't have to tell me. You've been a hard worker ever since you was a little kid. Smart too. Why...."

"But you taught me all that stuff," said Jesse.

"Yeah, maybe...." said Tom. "But you don't know how hard I had to keep working just to keep on teaching you new things. You was always so close behind me, I had to run to keep ahead."

"And I was running just to catch up."

"And I was running just to try to keep ahead," Tom said laughingly.

"Oh geez," said Jesse, "Tom, that sounds so great. I'd be getting out, just like you."

"No," corrected Tom, " you'd be getting out better than me. I'm out for a while but when I finish the Army, don't know where I'll be. You'd be getting out for good, for sure."

They both sat silently for a minute, each thinking to themselves what getting out meant.

Jesse had thought a long while and then had said, "And the part about mom?"

"Well," Tom said. "Mom's an alcoholic."

The words went through Jesse like a shiver. He wanted to protest. It seemed like such an awful thing to say. And here it was Tom calling his own mother that.

"But . . ." Jesse had started to say.

"I learned that in the Army," Tom had continued. "I mean I knew she got drunk a lot. And I knew she liked it a lot but I guess I never thought of her as having a disease."

There was something else strange Tom was saying—that his mother was sick; had a disease. Jesse tried to make sense out of it. He'd seen people on the streets and in his neighborhood drunk all his life. Everything from the winos down by the warehouses to the loud-mouth drunks on the door steps. And when his mother was drunk, she was as drunk as any of them but she was drunk from drinking a bottle, not sick with an illness.

"Not everybody who drinks gets to be an alcoholic. It's sort of like diabetes. If someone in your family had it, the more likely you're gonna get it. But it can skip (like from a grandfather or grandmother to a granddaughter or grandson) and miss all the people in between. But if it's in your family, then it's there and you better watch out."

"Where'd you get that, Tom?" Jesse had asked. It all seemed so strange. Even though it was his brother telling him, it was still hard to believe.

"They told us about that in the Army. See, when you go overseas and you don't have no family near by and you don't know anybody, one of the things most of the dudes do is drink. They go out and drink when they get a chance."

"Did you?" asked Jesse.

"No, I told you. I knew I had a special purpose for the

money I was getting. That money had to come back home, come right to this house."

"You never did forget us," Jesse had said, the tears coming to his eyes.

"No," Tom had said quietly. "I never did. Did you think I would?"

Jesse had hesitated. "No, I guess not. But when we didn't hear from you it was kinda hard to keep on believin'."

"Well, it took me a while to get straightened out what I wanted. You know when I left here I just wanted to get away so bad. Like I didn't care whether I ever came back. And then when you get off on your own, you get mixed up with all different kinds of people and things and you start thinking about belonging. And though I didn't want to belong here no more, I did have kin. And as bad or good as they are, kin are somebody special.

"There's lot of people out there in the world," Tom had continued. "Don't none of 'em really care about you. Least not like 'kin'. And I kept thinking: In all this world I got a mother and I got a brother. I'm out here and life is a lot better for me. But they're there. And life isn't ever gonna change for them. Ain't no miracles gonna come down our street. If anything is ever gonna change for them, I gotta do the changing. Then I decided that was what I was gonna do. I was gonna save all the money I made and try to do some changing."

Jesse had listened carefully throughout Tom's explanation.

"So you see," finished Tom. "To begin with, there weren't no use in writing because I didn't have nothing to say. Even when I found out where I was going, there wasn't nothin' to say, just something to do and I just had to do it. So here I am just trying to do it. Trouble is, it isn't enough to do everything. It's gotta be one or the other."

Jesse had thought about what Tom had said a long time. He wanted out as bad as Tom had wanted out. Geez, did he want out.

"Well," Tom had continued, "it was easy to understand what I could do for you. Matter of fact, I told you I learned about that place before I even got out of the States. But when I was over there, I understood mom was an alcoholic and had a disease and then I knew what I could do for her. I could try to get her help."

Although not everyone is willing to call alcoholism a disease, there is general agreement it is an illness. However, it is an illness which can be kept under control as long as alcohol is not consumed. Alcoholics are well aware of this fact when they say, "One is too many and a thousand is not enough." Some research has been done on teaching alcoholics to drink in a controlled or social way. These treatment approaches are experimental as yet and are not recommended.

It is important to note, however, that alcoholism is associated with or causative in relation to a wide range of physical disorders, many of which are not reversible. Advanced alcoholism leads to gastritis, ulcers, pancreatitis, hepatitis, heart disease. Cirrhosis (scarring of the liver) ranks as the sixth most common cause of death in the United States with up to ninety-five percent of these cases considered to be alcohol-related. Years of too much alcohol can damage the brain to the point that normal functioning is impossible. Alcohol consumption can also physically harm the life of another if alcohol is consumed during pregnancy. Infants born with the fetal-alcohol syndrome may have birth defects as well as suffer the pains of withdrawal from alcohol.

Jesse had struggled again with the idea his mom had a disease.

"See, first I thought I might try to get her a better house, or some furniture, or give her a vacation trip—something like that," Tom had said. "But even then I wasn't sure that'd change all that much for her. Then the more I began to think the more I understood why. As long as she's sick, nothing is going to change for her. She's got to get well first."

Jesse had mulled over what Tom was saying. He did care for his mom. He cared for her in a strange way though. He could walk out on her, he thought, just like Tom could. He could just go out the door and keep going. He knew he could. And it wasn't just that she'd taken his money and lost it. It was, well, the way she'd become. Sloppy. Didn't care about herself. Getting her pleasure from a bottle rather than learning anything or doing anything. Making promises and never keeping them. She was the way he didn't want to be all his life.

But then as he thought about how she was, he knew Tom was right. She was sick. She couldn't help herself any more than you could help yourself when you had a cold. No amount of will power was going to make you get rid of a cold. You just kinda had to ride it out. Only with his mom's disease, riding it out didn't work. You just couldn't ever get better. It just hung on and on.

"So, I asked about treatment for mom and they told me about all different kinds. But mainly she's got to get help, get off alcohol, and then get some more help. And she's going to need help for a long time."

The first phase of helping a person is enabling him or her to recognize that a problem exists. Sometimes this happens to the person on his own when he "hits bottom." This means life itself becomes so unbearable that the alcoholic realizes he has a problem and reaches out for help. Another way people are made aware of their problem is through "confrontation." Family members and others—teachers, friends, employers, co-workers—share with the alcoholic how his or her behavior has affected them. Confrontation can take many forms but the key to its success is caring and responsibility. Generally it is best carried out with professional guidance.

The next step is a process of separating the person from alcohol. Detoxification is not considered to be treatment for alcoholism. During the "detox" the alcoholic recovers from the ill effects of alcohol poisoning. However, detoxification can be a major step in the recovery process.

The third phase of helping an alcoholic is rehabilitation. This can be done on an inpatient basis where the person stays in a private hospital, special clinic, or mental health care facility. Some of the programs are time limited to four, six, or eight weeks of treatments. Others have patients stay until they seem ready to leave and remain sober.

It can also be done on an outpatient basis. Outpatient services for an alcoholic can be provided in a mental health clinic or a psychiatric hospital. Various alcoholism centers provide one-to-one, family, and group counseling. Many people who use inpatient care are then transferred to outpatient care programs.

A wide variety of services may be needed in the third phase of helping an alcoholic. A person may need help in the area of housing, financial assistance, job training, marital counseling, and so forth. Some people need special places to live such as halfway houses or placement with a family to permit them to return gradually to full participation in community life.

"The doctor can see you now." The voice of the receptionist cut into Jesse's thoughts. Jesse looked at his brother. How long he been lost in his thoughts?

The two brothers got up and went into the doctor's office.

"Well," said the doctor motioning them to sit down. "As you know, I saw your mother yesterday for an examination. She is willing to undergo the treatment. But I want you to know I'm not absolutely sure she understands what it's all about and how hard it's going to be. And I don't mean just going through detoxification but staying alcohol free."

Tom spoke. "This is really an important decision not just for our mother, but for us, particularly for my brother here. I guess we gotta understand a little better what you're saying."

"OK," said the doctor. "Let me just kind of walk you through what can happen when someone tries to get off alcohol. Even for someone who is not a long-term drinker, getting off alcohol can cause at least mild symptoms—like feeling irritable, rapid heartbeat, sweating, shaking, insomnia, muscle weakness, the runs, nausea and vomiting. For someone like your mother, for a heavy drinker, these symptoms can be severe, not knowing where one is, being out of one's head, seeing things that are not there, frantic feelings, and seizures. We call these severe symptoms, the D.T.'s or delirium tremens. It's an awful thing for anyone to go through and possibly can lead to death—that's why withdrawal from alcohol is a serious matter and should be done under medical care."

Jesse suddenly remembered a morning he had seen a wino sitting on some steps. The guy had fallen off onto his head. Jesse had heard such a crack he had thought the guy's head would have cracked open. But it was like the guy didn't feel a thing. He seemed to be OK. However, that night when Jesse had passed by the same spot, the guy was lying on the ground in spasms like a dog running in his sleep. An ambulance came for him.

"But isn't there anything you can do?" Jesse blurted out, that horrible image still in his mind.

"Yes," said the doctor. "That's why your mother will have to come to the center here. Six hours after having her last drink, your mother will begin to have some of those mild symptoms we talked about. It will be our job to prevent those major symptoms from happening. We'll do that with drugs. The drugs—we call it chemical sedation—are needed so that the body can begin to gradually cope without alcohol. After a couple days or a week, these drugs will be given in smaller and smaller amounts until your mother is just on vitamins. We give all patients the vitamins since most people who are alcoholics don't eat right and generally have a vitamin lack. During the rest of the time your mother is here, we will work on diet and nutrition. But more important than that, your mother will be involved in recreation and therapy."

The doctor paused, giving time for Tom and Jesse to digest what he had said and to ask questions.

"The recreation is to help people relax and give them a new sense of their body. The therapy is to help them realize they have a problem and suggest ways they can cope."

"But . . ." Jesse started to say. Then his voice faded out.

"It's hard for us to understand," said the doctor. "To family and friends it is all too clear what alcohol has done to the person's life. But most often the person himself can't see it."

Jesse thought back about his mother. He remembered a time in her life when she had looked pretty good, when she had taken care of herself. She had had that job working for that lady who was really good to her and to them. He remembered her going out early every morning so she could get done and home by the time he and Tom came home from school. Sometimes the lady would give her clothes for them and at holiday time she sent along a turkey or a tree or something. His mom had held her head up then. Now there wasn't nobody going to hire his mother, not even that nice lady. And his mom didn't never hold up her head any more.

Jesse sighed. And the doctor was right. Much as he pleaded with his mom to stop drinking, much as he tried to tell her what was happening to her, she couldn't see it. He winced as he remembered when she had thrown the bottle at him. She didn't know what she was doing. She couldn't see that. Didn't even remember the next morning she had done it. She'd asked him if he had been in a fight with somebody and warned him not to fight again.

At high levels, alcohol has a toxic effect on the brain which shuts down normal memory functioning. The affected person continues to do many things but the brain loses its ability to store memory of what is going on. It is called "blacking out." This can go on for days or sometimes a week.

"You see," the doctor went on, "unless the person can truly begin to understand what alcohol has done to their life, they aren't ever going to change. While they are here, we try to have them share their feelings and their lives with others who have had the same problems. We try to help them see that they are not alone, that this is a problem for many people, and that if they want their lives to be different, they have to begin to take a different kind of responsibility for themselves."

Tom nodded. "And when she leaves here?"

"Well," said the doctor, looking at Tom's uniform, "since I guess you will be away, a lot of responsibility is going to fall on your brother."

Jesse started slightly. A questioning look crossed his face.

"Family support is very important to the recovering alcoholic. For a person to get better they have to change much of what they think and do. They need support from their family to do that. The person has to be helped not to dwell on the past—not to bemoan what alcohol or other events have done to their life. But they also just can't pretend it never happened. Many alcoholics think they are cured or just one drink won't matter. Before they know it, they are right back where they started from. Although your mom's sobriety is her responsibility, support from you, Jesse, will be important."

Jesse sighed. He thought of how much he had begged his mother not to drink and her broken promises.

"What's the matter, Jesse?" the doctor asked.

"I've told her over and over again. I said, 'Mom, please don't. You've had enough. Please don't drink,' and she promises and promises and promises and then always goes back and does it." His shoulders shook with dispair as he said it.

"That's why we don't leave you or your mother out there alone, Jesse," the doctor said. "There's a group called Alateen. You ever heard of it?"

Jesse shook his head 'no.'

"Well, Alateen is an organization set up to help teenagers who have an alcoholic in their family."

"I'm not an alcoholic," said Jesse, startled.

"No," said the doctor. "You misunderstood. Alateen is for teens who have someone else in their family who is an alcoholic. It's not for teens who are alcoholics themselves. OK?"

"OK," said Jesse feeling better again.

The doctor continued. "You will be given an opportunity, in fact, asked if you would go to their meetings. Other young people who have an alcoholic in their family will be there too. You'll find out the broken promises have happened to other young people too. You'll find that having someone who's an alcoholic in the family affects not just their life but yours. You can learn more about the disease of alcoholism and maybe some important ways that you can help support your mother as she tries to recover, without harming your own life."

Jesse listened carefully. Up to now he had thought of his

mother as just messing up her own life. It flashed across him now that that just wasn't true. She was messing up his life too. Even as he sat here in the doctor's office he was giving up getting to go to a special school, get out, be somebody. His mother was taking away the biggest chance he might ever have in his whole life. She was messing up his life. All of a sudden he was very angry at his mother. He wanted to strike out, shake her, and tell her how much she was doing to him.

The doctor may have seen the expression on Jesse's face because he added, "Living with a sick person is not easy. Living with a person who is recovering is not easy either. Sometimes one can expect too much from them too soon. They may have been a burden before but they become a different kind of burden when they are getting better. It's important to see what your role is. Otherwise you might try to take on too much. They are responsible for their own life. At the same time, let me stress, family support is very important to the likelihood of your mother's getting better."

Recent long-term studies show that abstinence from alcohol is the cornerstone of recovery for the alcoholic. These studies also affirm the importance of A.A. participation. Alcoholics Anonymous is a national organization which provides opportunities for alcoholics to help themselves through sharing common problems. Al-Anon is a self-help movement which arose as a movement parallel to, but separate from, (AA) Alcoholics Anonymous. Over 5,000 Al-Anon groups now exist throughout the world. The relatives of alcoholics find fellowship in Al-Anon which helps them deal with the fact of having an alcoholic in their lives. Alateen is a similar self-help movement which allows children of alcoholics to gain understanding and support for their dilemma through association with one another.

"That's something I wanted to ask you about again," Tom said. "Remember I asked you what was the chances of my mother getting better?"

"Well, that's not really predictable," said the doctor, "there are so many factors."

"No," said Tom. "You don't understand. We got a special reason for wanting to know. My brother here is giving up something pretty important to him—something very important to him for my mother to come here. If she's not going to be cured. . . . If he's going to do all this, and then she's just the same, well, you see, he . . . we . . . might not want to do it. It's a pretty important decision for him . . . us."

"Well," said the doctor studying them both, "I can see you're looking for more of an answer than perhaps I can give you."

Jesse and Tom sat silently.

The doctor turned around in his chair and looked out the window for a minute as if weighing something. "The fact that we have so many alcoholics in the United States shows how hard it is for people to be helped," he finally said. "Indeed there is no such thing as a cure anyway. Alcohol is everywhere," he added. "It seems to be so much a part of our lives. It is hard for a person who has had a life style that includes alcohol to suddenly switch to one that doesn't."

He paused. "I'm going to say some things to you now that maybe I shouldn't. . . . Your mom doesn't have a lot of job skills, she isn't married right now, she doesn't seem to be interested in the church or any other group. She's got to make a real effort to get out and get into something or else she'll have less than a fifty/fifty chance of making it."

"However," the doctor continued, "on the other hand, she has got you two—particularly you, Jesse, since you're at home. And having a caring family can be a powerful influence. She's very lucky that way."

Something the doctor said sounded like other words Jesse had heard just recently. He struggled to remember. Slowly it came back to him, 'You get mixed up with all different kinds of people and things and you start thinking about belonging. And as bad or good as they are, kin are somebody special. There's a lot of people out there in the world. Don't none of 'em really care about you. Least not like kin.' Suddenly Jesse remembered. They were Tom's words trying to tell him something he'd learned.

Jesse sat up straight. Yep, his mom did have somebody.

She did have him. And he'd be there when she needed him—even if it didn't work. She could count on him. Just like he had counted on Tom. And Tom had come home, caring. And he'd stay home, caring. He would just have to put off thinking of the big future for a while—being somebody—maybe next year or the year after.

"Any more questions?" the doctor asked. Then he added, "we did discuss on the phone the first time you called that this was a private care facility and you could get less expensive care elsewhere."

"Yes," said Tom. "But I heard good things about this place and if she comes, I want her to come here. And you told me how much it was and I got that money. I just have to check again with my brother and see what he wants to do. We'll call you later after we talk it over one more time."

"Don't have to call later," said Jesse. "Mom's coming here."

"You sure?" said Tom.

"Yes, I'm sure," said Jesse.

"Well, then," said the doctor. "I'll make arrangements for your mother to enter on Monday."

They shook hands with the doctor and then went out.

Once outside on the street, Tom turned to Jesse. "Since I won't be here on Monday, I want to give this to you right now. You're the one in charge from here on." He pulled a money order out of his pocket and handed it to Jesse. Jesse took it, looked at it, and then folded it up and put it in his pocket.

"I wish I could stay," said Tom, "but you know they only gave me a week and I've got to report back Sunday night."

"I know," Jesse said.

"You OK?" Tom asked, putting his hands on both Jesse's shoulders.

Jesse looked at Tom's face. He could tell Tom was still worried about his giving up the special school.

Jesse's mind flashed back. He saw himself sneaking out of the house. He saw himself swinging off the back porch going down to see the guys. He saw himself hanging around the playground so he wouldn't have to go home. He saw himself staying in his room late so he wouldn't have to face his mother in the morning. He saw himself as the kid he was, just running away from what it was like at home, trying to wriggle under, in, out, and around like it was at home. Then the image changed. He pictured himself walking up to the back door, opening it and walking in, straight in, with his shoulders square. And suddenly he didn't feel like that kid. It was as if something really strange was going on inside that didn't make getting out so important at the moment.

"Hey man," said Jesse suddenly. "I'm your brother, ain't I? In case you haven't noticed, you better start running. I just had a sudden feeling I'm starting to catch up again."

14 ✌ Christine—Choices

Christine held the small bouquet of flowers nervously in her hand. She paused at the door to Sandra's hospital room. Sandra's bandages were going to be off her face for the first time. Christine wondered how she could control her reaction if it was really bad. Sandra had already warned Christine the doctors had said she would need some plastic surgery on her face. Christine took a deep breath and walked in. Sandra was sitting on the side of her bed with her back to Christine.

"Hi" said Christine. "Is it OK to come in?"

"Sure," said Sandra turning around.

Christine caught her breath. Sandra had an ugly purple blue scar down one side of her face and her skin seemed to be strangely sunken in like part of her face was gone underneath. There was still a patch over one eye.

Sandra noticed Christine's expression.

"Oh, that's right. You haven't seen it. Well, here it is. I'm not exactly what you'd call your darling cheer leader type any more."

Christine didn't know what to say. There was an uncomfortable silence.

"Hey, I'm sorry." Sandra spoke first. "I'm really not that

bitter. I'm lucky to be alive. I know that. The doctor has said with some plastic surgery they can fill this out where my facial bones were shattered and although I'll have a scar, they can make it a much better looking one. With makeup, the doctor says, it won't stand out—still be noticeable, but won't stand out." Sandra paused. "But...."

Christine moved closer to the bed sensing her friend was especially troubled.

"Oh Christine," Sandra said suddenly. "They still don't know about my eye. They think they may have to take it out and give me a glass eye." Sandra dropped her head and her voice quavered. "A glass eye. I'm going to have to go through life with a stupid glass eye that will just stare straight ahead." A sob escaped her.

Christine sat down on the bed next to her friend. She put her arm around her.

"Oh Sandra," she said. "I'm so sorry."

Sandra let several more sobs escape her. Then she straightened her shoulders, slowly swung her feet up on the bed, and gradually pushed herself back so that she was sitting against the head of the bed. "I'm sorry I did that," she said sniffing and reaching for a Kleenex. "I don't know why I burst out about it. I thought I'd gotten it all out of my system."

"Do you want me to go?" said Christine.

"No, stay," said Sandra. She tossed her Kleenex in the waste paper basket. As she did she noticed the bouquet. "Oh flowers," she said. "You brought me flowers. How nice. There's a vase down under this stand. Would you put them in water for me?"

Christine reached down and opened the hospital bedstand and took out a vase.

"Water's in the john," Sandra said motioning toward the bathroom. "But say," she added, "shouldn't I be giving you flowers? Isn't it your birthday?"

"Yes," said Christine. "I finally made sixteen. Happy birthday to me," she sang and then drowned out the rest by running water into the vase.

"You having a party?" Sandra asked when the water was off.

"No," said Christine. She frowned. It struck her as odd that Sandra should have asked that. Didn't Sandra realize how much Christine's life had changed since the car crash. But then, Christine reasoned, this was Sandra's second month in the hospital. Sandra undoubtedly assumed everyone else's life was the same and only hers had changed.

"No," said Christine more firmly. "However, my mom and dad are picking me up here and going to take me out to lunch with Kay. You remember Kay from our dance class. It's Kay's birthday too, so we're going to have a double celebration."

"How come they're taking you to lunch, not dinner?" asked Sandra smoothing her covers.

"Oh, dad's going out of town this evening." Christine was surprised she could talk about it without sounding bitter or angry. Birthdays had always been important in her family. At one time she would have been crushed not to have had a special birthday dinner with her family. Now, however, she really didn't care so much. Even when her family was home, she liked to spend time by herself in her room reading or thinking.

"There," she put the flowers on the stand and gave them a final arrangement.

"Christine, you've been great about coming to the hospital," Sandra said as Christine plopped into the chair next to her bed.

"Sure," said Christine.

"No," said Sandra. "I really mean it. Some of the other kids have come but you've come all the time."

"Why shouldn't I?" said Christine.

"Well," said Sandra, "I don't know." Then she said, "Yes, I do know. I mean I'm not sure I would have. I was pretty self-centered, you know. I thought looks and going out with those boys and drinking and having sex was really what everything was all about."

Sandra looked at Christine for understanding. "I mean

why, my God, when Mark asked me out that first time, I couldn't believe it. I forget exactly why he told me he did it. I mean later on he said it was because some of the boys had said the sophomores had cuter girls than the senior class and I was the cutest cheer leader or something and he sorta did it on a bet. That was before we got to know each other. I mean we really liked each other when we started going out." Sandra paused and smiled.

"And I thought, wow, it was so grown up to be going out with him and doing all those things. I just didn't feel a part of our class any more. I mean if some girl in our class had gotten in an accident, I would have thought 'too bad' and just gone about my business. . . . I couldn't have cared less."

Christine winced as she remembered her angry quarrel with Kay. Kay had said Christine didn't care about anyone any more. And Christine winced again as she remembered calling her friend jealous for saying it.

"I just got so self-centered," said Sandra. "Now that I think back, it's as if I became a different person after I met Mark. I just couldn't wait to get with those kids and start drinking to feel mellow or high or whatever. Now that I think about it, half the stuff I was feeling was coming from a piece of paper or out of a bottle. I didn't have room for a lot of real feelings of my own." Sandra seemed to fumble for what more to say.

"I know what you mean," said Christine helping her out. "God, when I think how much I had started to drink. I wasn't an alcoholic or anything. But I wanted to get those feelings more and more. I was even stealing liquor at home."

"Were you?" Sandra seemed surprised. "I didn't know that." Then she added seriously, "But you see that's all part of it. Even though we were running around together, I didn't really get to know you any better. I didn't know what was going on with you. And what's more I didn't care. Do you understand what I'm trying to say? I was so wound up in myself and the alcohol and the kids, I didn't care about anyone but me."

"I guess it was the same with me," said Christine, "maybe

not quite as much but pretty much the same."

"But now . . ." Sandra paused. "Now it's different. I can't be glad this happened. God, I wish it hadn't. And yet it's made me see things so differently. . . . Even . . ." she added wryly, "with my one eye."

When Christine didn't say anything, Sandra continued. "Every day I used to get up and think: When am I going to see Mark next, when am I going to drink next, where are we going to go next, what's the crowd doing next? And nothing was ever more than a day or a weekend ahead, if you know what I mean. I mean I just lived from drink to drink and party to party and smoke to smoke."

"I know," said Christine. "I didn't go to ballet much. My grades got awful. At least you kept being a cheer leader. I quit that."

"Well," said Sandra. "Now all of a sudden I've started to think differently—more than a day or so at a time. I think. . . . You know, I always thought 'I will get out of high school and I will go to college.' But now it just isn't I will go to college, it's will I go to college? And if I go to college, what do I really want to try to learn? and what do I really want to try to do there? I think, 'who do I really want to get to know and why? What does that person have to offer me and what do I have to offer them?' "

Christine sat quietly. "I'm sorry about Mark," she finally said.

Sandra rested her head back on the pillow. "I've had a lot of time to think about that too," she said. "I mean, when someone dies who's your own age or near your own age, well, it just doesn't seem like it could be real, that it could happen. I mean, you always think about old people dying but not someone your own age, not someone you know."

"Yes," Christine said.

"And when I heard Mark was dead I thought I would die. I thought he was the most important person in the world to me. I thought I loved him more than anything. But then, you know, the more it became real to me that he was really dead, the more I thought about him differently." Sandra sat forward and looked at Christine. "You knew Mark and I were having sex?"

Christine nodded. "I thought you were."

"Well, Mark and I had sex during the party the night of the accident. And so at first I thought, well maybe I'll be pregnant and then I'll have something to remember him by—this great love, you know. And then, of course I wasn't. And then I started to think, well, what if I had been? It would really have been hard to manage without a husband, without a father for the baby."

Sandra lay back still looking at Christine. "And then you know what I thought? I thought well what if Mark were alive, how would it have been then? And you know what I realized for the first time? I didn't want to have a baby by Mark. Mark was into everything for good times. He wouldn't have been interested in taking care of me and a baby. As a matter of fact, Mark didn't have the foggiest idea of what he was going to do in life. I mean he was just like I was, going from one drink to one party to one smoke. And the more I thought about it, the more I realized that's mostly what we had in common. If you had taken the parties and grass and booze away, we wouldn't have known how to get along together." Sandra stopped. "Christine, I'm sorry. I'm just talking on and on."

"No, go on," said Christine. "I'm interested. I understand what you're saying."

Sandra continued. "And it's not that I'm not all for having a good time. Don't get me wrong. I mean the accident hasn't converted me into a nun or anything. It's just that, well, let's face it, we were dumb to be doing all that stuff. The pot probably wasn't good for our brains. If I'd gotten VD or pregnant, that wouldn't have been good for my body. And the alcohol wasn't good for our stomachs or livers or whatever. And we were dumb to be doing it when we didn't know how to handle it."

Christine nodded. "I know I felt so grown up, I thought I was just the neatest person in the world. And I thought I could do anything just about, and it would be OK."

"That's it," said Sandra. "It wasn't so much the doing it. We could have done the same thing—drank, smoked, had sex—well, maybe a little less of it all—if we had some idea of what we were getting into. We just never knew the fact was, it was going to change us by just spending our time doing that, that there were risks to it. . . ." Sandra fumbled for what to say. "I mean life is a risk. But it was like I didn't know it then. It was like. . . ." She started again. "Let me put it this way; Christine, if you had said to me: Sandra, you're going to be an alcoholic, or you're going to be pregnant, or you're going to get killed in a car accident I would have said to you, 'Oh no, it can't happen to me.' And I would have believed it."

"That's it!" Sandra looked surprised at what she had just said, then said again, "That's it! That's the whole difference I've been trying to tell you. I've just said it. All of a sudden, that is what I've discovered. *It can happen to me.*"

Both girls looked at one another trying to grasp the full meaning of what Sandra was saying.

Christine finally said, "I do know what you mean. It's like all of a sudden you discover that you've just been letting things happen to you even when you thought you were making them happen. And you suddenly discover you've got a lot more to do with life than you thought. And it's like all of a sudden you discover that there's a choice to everything and by just letting things happen, you're really making a choice."

"Exactly," said Sandra.

"I don't think anyone else would know what we were talking about, do you?" said Christine half smiling.

"Probably not," said Sandra grinning back. "But then again, maybe some of them would but I've just never taken the time to find out."

"Or couldn't find out because you didn't know it yourself to find out," replied Christine.

All of a sudden both girls laughed at how involved their conversation had become.

"When is a rose a rose a rose is a rosa a rose . . ." said Sandra gaily. Then she quickly added, "Oh thank you for coming." She giggled. "Really, I meant what I said when I said. . . ." She burst out laughing. "Oh, you know about your coming when your coming when you come." She couldn't finish because she was laughing so much. She tossed her head back.

Christine was laughing too.

All of a sudden Sandra clutched at the patch over her eye and let out a scream.

Christine jumped out of her chair, scared. "Sandra, what is it?"

Sandra did not respond. "Oh," she cried, bending forward and grabbing frantically at the patch. "Oh my God, it hurts."

Christine looked at Sandra. She quickly reached over Sandra's bed and pulled the nurse's cord. Sandra screamed again and rocked backward holding her eye.

A voice over the intercom said "May I help. . . ." The rest of the words were drowned out by Sandra's cries.

"Come quick!" Christine yelled. She reached over and grabbed Sandra's twisting body to keep her from falling out of bed.

A doctor and two nurses rushed into the room. They brushed Christine aside and leaned over Sandra.

Another nurse came in. She put her arm around Christine's shoulder. "Come, I think you better go now." She led Christine toward the door.

"What's the matter with her?" Christine asked looking back toward the bed. She couldn't see Sandra because of the nurses and doctors.

"What's the matter with her?" Christine asked again when she was outside.

"I don't know," said the nurse. "But her eye is damaged and maybe she's having increased pressure on the optic nerve. Sometimes with eye injuries it's hard to know how they'll go."

"Oh," said Christine, "we were laughing." She felt panicked. "I shouldn't have made her laugh."

"There, there, don't think such a thing," said the nurse guiding her down the hall. "Nothing you did had anything to do with what's going on with her. If she was not supposed to laugh, the doctor would have told her. Laughter had nothing to do with it. Now don't worry. Nothing you did had anything to do with what's going on with her."

The nurse paused with Christine by the elevator. "Call back this afternoon and you can find out how she is. Don't worry. It will be OK. And remember," she said comfortingly, "nothing you did had anything to do with what's going on with her."

The elevator door opened. All the way down to the first floor the nurse's words kept echoing in Christine's mind. "Nothing you did." But, Christine thought, I saw the way Mark drove when he drank. On the way back from the horseback ride I saw it and I didn't say anything to Sandra. I saw him leave other parties and I never told her I thought it was dangerous for her to keep riding with him. I knew they'd had a lot to drink at Loretta Banks' birthday party. I didn't say anything. I never said to Sandra, Don't ride with him, ride with us. It doesn't matter whether or not she would have listened. I know I never tried to tell her. I do have *everything* to do with what's going on with Sandra.

The elevator door opened and Christine walked slowly through the hospital lobby and pushed open the main door. She looked around. Her father's car was parked near the entrance. Kay was leaning out of the back seat window waving at her.

Half-dreamlike, Christine moved to the car. She opened the back door and started to climb in.

"Hey" her dad said enthusiastically. "We were just talking with Kay and we thought we'd all go over to that new Polynesian restaurant to celebrate your birthdays. Your mom tells me they have the most delicious rum drinks anyone ever tasted—sort of like pop but with a real kick. And now that you're sixteen," he added grandly, "I think both of you are old enough to celebrate your birthday with a little drink."

Christine hesitated. Then she slowly lowered herself into the back seat.

"She's going to go through life with a glass eye," she mumbled.

"Well, you can have a glass of cider if that's what you want dear," her mother said. "But the rum drinks really are delicious."

"A glass eye," Christine said louder. "A glass eye," she said again. "Don't you hear me?" she suddenly screamed. "She's going to go through life with a glass eye!"

Christine tore open the car door and raced down the hospital driveway.

Everyone in the car turned and stared after her as if they thought she'd gone mad.

"Well," her father finally said with a shrug, "maybe she had her heart set on going someplace else."

A tragic experience may lead a heavy drinker to give up alcohol. Some can do this successfully without professional help while many find it impossible to quit drinking in spite of their resolutions—simply saying one is not an alcoholic does not make it so.

15 ~ Penni—Choices

"Go on, Penni, tell us what happened," said a boy. Penni was sitting in a group of young people telling about the day she had decided to steal liquor from the fourth floor apartment in her building. She went on with her explanation.

"Well, the lady in the apartment below had apparently heard me walking around and called the police. Of course, they didn't know it was me. I guess they thought it was a real burglar."

"But you were a real burglar, weren't you Penni?" one of the other kids asked.

Penni paused. She knew the question wasn't meant in a mean way. Penni looked around at the group of kids. All the kids there had problems with alcohol too, and many had had worse experiences than she had.

"I guess you're right," Penni said. "It's so easy to twist your mind around and think what you're doing isn't really what you're doing. Actually they did tell my mom and dad when they came down to the jail to get me that I could be charged with breaking and entering, theft, and I don't know what else. So I guess I really was a thief."

The alcoholic who becomes involved in criminal activity—shoplifting, burglary, dealing in drugs, and so forth—when caught is prosecuted and will have to carry any conviction as part of his or her permanent record. Most applications for jobs, drivers licenses, loans, and so forth—have questions having to do with whether or not the person was ever arrested and whether or not they ever were convicted of a crime. Young offenders are often required to become involved in a juvenile rehabilitation program. If it is clear that the criminal activity was alcohol-related, participation in an alcohol treatment program may be required instead of offender rehabilitation.

"You would have thought I would have faced up to being an alcoholic then," Penni continued. Penni was surprised. Every time she spoke about herself as an alcoholic it got easier. "But I didn't. My parents wouldn't believe it either. After they got me off so I wouldn't have to go to jail or anything, they just said that we'd all forget about what had happened. But then they caught me drunk about a month later. So they sent me to a psychiatrist."

"That do any good?" one of the kids asked.

"Well, probably not for me. But it did for my parents. See, they wanted to pretend nothing was wrong. But he just flat out told them that my main problem was not a mental one but a drinking one. He said regardless of whether or not I could use some mental help, I first had to get some help for my drinking."

"What happened then?"

"Oh, not much. I think my parents were ashamed. They tried to give me lots of attention and all that stuff. They were really worried but they didn't know what to do."

Being an alcoholic carries a great deal of stigma with it and a family may not want to admit they may have a member or several members who have this disease. They may prefer to deny it. Parents may say "So my kid drinks, don't they all these days?" Or parents can go for months or years and not even be aware of what is happening because they maintain so much distance from their child. Because they refuse to face the fact that their child has a problem, parents can actually support the alcohol habit—in essence becoming "enablers." They may make excuses for their child, bail him or her out of jail, pay his or her bills, and many other things to help their child out of short-term crises but never face up to the long-term drinking problem. As this pattern progresses, the family itself becomes so wrapped into the alcoholism that the entire family unit needs help in facing the problem and in learning new ways of coping with the illness. Professionals can help families do this as well as Al-Anon and other self-help groups.

"So, what finally got you to face up to the fact that you were an alcoholic, Penni?" someone asked.

"My brother," Penni replied.

"What d'you mean?"

"Well, I guess my parents were so busy with my problem, they didn't notice that Freddie had one too. But I knew.

"Anyway, one day Freddie didn't come home from elementary school on time. And it was one of those rainy yicky days so I told my mother I'd go look for him. And I went all the way over to his school and I still didn't see him. I checked in the school and there wasn't anyone there and I was just about to give up, when. . . . Anyway, I saw this kid's coat thrown down in the mud by the gym door. And it was the same color as Freddie's. And so I went over."

Penni paused and swallowed. "And then I saw that it wasn't just a coat lying in the mud, it was a kid. And the kid had a bottle in his hand and he'd passed out right there in the mud and the rain." Penni winced as she remembered. "And that kid lying there in the mud was Freddie. And somehow it was then that I saw myself. It was sure as if it were me lying there in the mud. And then I knew I had to get help for Freddie and I had to get help for me."

"Well, how's Freddie doing now?"

"Oh, he's doing pretty good. He hadn't been drinking as long or as much as I had. My parents have him in a different school and they got him into special things he likes doing. Yah, he's doing pretty good."

"And how you doing, Penni?"

"Me, well, I don't know. When I first started to come here,

I felt strange. I mean it really takes something to say to yourself you're an alcoholic and you can't stop. I always thought I could . . . you know what I mean? Anyway the hardest thing for me was giving up my friends at the Mall. It just left me feeling all alone not to see those kids any more. Yet talking with you kids and others here showed me I couldn't go with them and not drink."

"Well, we are your friends, Penni."

"I know," said Penni, "and the kids here are great. But you know, you're not from my neighborhood and it's not like well, you know. . . ."

"Yeah, we know," said one boy. "I felt all alone too. Sometimes I still do."

"I think that's why I went back to drinking last month," Penni said. "You know, I felt lonely. I didn't feel much like I was anybody and I just wanted to be part of everything again. I thought I could have just one drink, you know, and well, some of you were here when I came back two weeks ago. I was in pretty bad shape. I couldn't stop at one, I couldn't stop at two, or even three, or four. Once I had started back, that was all I wanted. I can't remember much of what happened. I don't even know which of my friends I saw and which ones I didn't see."

When an alcoholic who is recovering drinks, it is called a "slip." "Slips" come for most alcoholics at one time or another and should not be viewed as failure. They should be viewed as part of the illness and obstacles to recovery. "Slips" are crises to be coped with—the goal should be to make them as short and involve as little drinking as possible. There are as many reasons why alcoholics slip as why they become alcoholics in the first place. The important thing is for the ill person and his or her family to realize that it is a crisis and there is a need for new efforts. The biggest problem in learning to live without alcohol is keeping personal awareness of the consequences of drinking. This is why self-help groups play such a significant role in maintaining sobriety. Often when kids stop going to self-help meetings somehow they "forget" they are alcoholic drinkers and begin to believe or hope

> *they may be able to drink socially. Also it is very hard for young people to give up their friends who abuse with drugs or drinking. Self-help groups say that the alcoholic and drug abuser must "change playgrounds and playmates" and this is one key to staying sober. The recovering alcoholic must find friends who are not preoccupied with drinking and in the beginning it's best to get involved with friends who don't drink at all. Self-help groups provide this atmosphere. A.A. (Alcoholics Anonymous) is one of the best known and most successful of these.*

A girl nodded her head in agreement. "I know," she said. "I always thought I could leave it alone anytime I wanted to. It was just that I never wanted to. But I found out different. The hard way. One night I found I'd do anything for it. And after that night, I guess I realized if I could do the things I did then, there wasn't anything going to stop me. I'd just go on being like that the rest of my life. I don't know what I would have done if it hadn't been for A.A. Has anyone here ever been to A.A.?"

"You know," another boy added, "you always think about A.A. as being an automobile club or something . . . somebody's stock rating. If you do think about it having to do with drinking, you think about it as being for grown-ups. I mean who thinks kids can become alcoholics?"

"WE DO!" the group called back.

"I mean. . . . Seriously," the guy asked, "did you ever think you could become an alcoholic before you became one?"

"No, we know what you mean," another girl said. "Probably none of us did."

"As for me," said another boy. "I thought I had a good excuse to drink. I mean I had it rough at home. Then some good things started happening at home and I didn't have that as an excuse any more so then I thought up other reasons to drink. I got so I could use anything as an excuse."

"Me too," said Penni. "I got so I drank because the sun came up and I drank because the sun went down. And if the sun didn't come up then it was cloudy and that gave me an excuse too. Actually, I'm lucky to be alive after the times I mixed downers with booze."

"It's really hard to stay chemical free," said one boy.

"Chemical free?" said Penni.

"Yeah, that's all alcohol is, is chemicals. That all all drugs are—chemicals. You pour these chemicals into your body and it makes your body go all crazy. You get your highs on chemicals."

"The trick is to switch to natural highs," someone else said.

"I still don't get many of those so-called 'natural' ones," said Penni.

"Yeah, I know," said the boy. "You could get them easy if you were a mountain climber or if you could bunk down on a roller coaster at the amusement park or something."

"You know, I didn't use to think there were many natural highs," one girl said. "But I can get one just listening to really terrific music with a stereo headset on."

"Actually I can get one running," another boy confessed.

"Running?" Penni asked.

"Yeah. But not just running, I mean I'm trying to be a miler and when you've been running for a while it really does something special to your body. I mean you can get a high from running—as a matter of fact while you are running."

"I can get a high from talking to someone," another girl said. "Not just regular talking but kind of a far-out free thinking sharing."

"But you still got to come down," said Penni.

"And it's still hard not being up," someone else said.

"But if life were a total 'up,' then there'd be no 'up,'" another voice added.

"Well, anyway, Penni," a girl said, "this afternoon you said you wanted us all to listen and try to help you. What can we do to help you?"

"I guess I want to know something you probably can't answer. Is there any.... I don't know how to say it. I liked what I became when I drank. I did all kinds of things I wouldn't have done as me. Now that I don't drink, I'm just me. And that isn't much. And I don't really know where I'm going and what's going to become of me. I don't really feel like a kid but everyone tells me I'm not grown up. Most of the people out there seem so 'nice' and I've done so many things that aren't 'nice.' I feel older than they are and younger too." Penni paused. "I just don't feel like I fit. And now that I can't drink to forget I don't fit, or I can't drink to make myself fit, I'm, well, I just guess I need help." Penni looked pleadingly at the group.

The group sat silently listening to what she had said.

Finally a girl spoke up.

"Penni, I really don't know what to say. I don't really know all the answers to those questions you asked. I can't help you with them. And I'm not sure anyone else can either. But I do know one thing. Alcohol is not the answer. Alcohol isn't it." Her voice was strong and firm as she said it again. "Alcohol isn't it."

Penni looked back at the group. She knew the girl was telling the truth.

"Alcohol isn't it," Penni said sadly, echoing her words. There was no answer—just a point to start from: *Alcohol isn't it.*

Resources

Where To Get More Information

National Clearinghouse for
Alcohol Information
Box 2345
Rockville, Maryland 20852

Alcoholics Anonymous
P.O. Box 459
Grand Central Station
New York, New York 10017

National Council on Alcoholism
733 Third Avenue
New York, New York 10017

Al-Anon Family Groups
115 East 23rd Street
New York, New York 10010

The Other Victims of Alcoholism
P.O. Box 921
Radio City Station
New York, New York 10019

Where To Get Help

In the yellow pages of your local phone directory, look under:
  Alcohol—Information and Treatment
  Clinics—Mental Health

In the white pages of your local phone directory, look under:
  Alcoholics Anonymous
  _____(Your state's name)_____ Council on Alcoholism